FIRST AID AFLOAT

www.fernhurstbo

FIRST
AID
AFLOAT

DR ROBERT HAWORTH

fernhurst
BOOKS

© Fernhurst Books 1993

First published 1993 and reprinted with corrections 1997 and 2001
by Fernhurst Books, Duke's Path, High Street, Arundel, West Sussex, BN18 9AJ, UK

Printed in China through World Print

British Library Cataloguing in Publication Data
A catalogue record for this book is available from the British Library

ISBN 0-906754-88-7

Acknowledgements
The author and publishers would like to thank Gerry Shepherd and
William Whitehead for providing boats for use during the photography
sessions, the crew of the Barmouth Lifeboat for demonstrating their
skills, Edward Jones for contriving such convincing 'injuries', and
Vicky Haworth, Gail Jones and Tim Davison for being model patients
in the photographs.

Photographic credits
All photographs by John Woodward except the following:
John Driscoll: page 91
Dr Robert Haworth: page 49
RFD Ltd: page 92
Yachting Monthly: page 90
Photographs printed by Julia Claxton

While every effort has been made to ensure that the advice
given in this book is correct, the publishers cannot accept any
liability for the outcome of any recommended treatment.

Edited and designed by John Woodward
Composition by Central Southern Typesetters, Eastbourne

CONTENTS

A medical emergency at sea is always more worrying than a similar emergency on land, because it takes much longer to get the casualty to medical aid. So it is essential that everyone who goes to sea in small craft has a working knowledge of First Aid. Indeed, anyone who goes to sea should regard First Aid as much a part of their training as seamanship and navigation.

This book will help. Before setting off, read pages 7 to 21 carefully: they will give you a basic understanding of emergency procedures. I also recommend that you read the sections on seasickness and on communicaions. The rest of the book is designed to be read in the event of injury or illness, giving you the information you need to act quickly and effectively, even if you have had no training in First Aid.

> **In the event of an accident consult the Golden Rules flowchart on the opposite page and follow the sequence of instructions given there.**

For specific injuries and illnesses consult the contents list on page 5, or the index at the back of the book.

The author, working under pressure.

GOLDEN RULES

1   Make sure that you are not putting yourself into danger by going to the casualty. When you are sure, approach the casualty coolly and thoughtfully.

2   Determine if the casualty is conscious or not.

3   Make sure that the casualty's airway is clear (page 10).

4   If the casualty is not breathing do artificial ventilation (page 12).

5   If the casualty has no circulation do external cardiac massage (page 14).

6   If the casualty is breathing and has a circulation but is unconscious, put him in the recovery position (page 10).

7   Look for bleeding and stop any you find (page 16).

8   Look for wounds, and treat them (page 34).

9   Check for fractures and immobilise any you find (pages 40–53).

10   Look for and treat any other injuries.

11   When you have attended to the casualty and you are aware of his condition decide if you require help. If you do turn to page 82: *Communications.*

A First Aid kit must be designed for the specific function that it is to be used for. We recommend three different kits which will be useful for different types of activity afloat.

Kit 1 is for dinghy sailors, day sailors, anglers, windsurfers and canoeists who will be able to get ashore and seek medical attention within four hours of the accident.

Kit 2 is for offshore sailors and fishermen who are well away from help and may have to look after a casualty for up to 48 hours before medical attention is available.

Kit 3 is for people making long ocean passages who will have to be self-dependent for a week or more.

Having the appropriate kit on board will not only help you control a situation until you get medical help. In many cases it will enable you to deal with the casualty yourself, so you do not have to give up your activity to seek help.

There are two other considerations for those undertaking long ocean passages. Firstly whether or not to take a very strong painkiller to deal with emergencies such as fractures when medical help may be days away. Most drugs which are used in medical practice to control severe pain such as morphine, pethidine etc are controlled by law and there may be difficulties with customs if you cross international boundaries. The best way to deal with this is to seek advice from a doctor when you know the distance that you are going to travel and for how long you will have to be self-dependent. When your doctor has advised you he will be able to issue a prescription for the drugs. Secondly you will need to carry antibiotics on long passages. I would advise one of the new 4-quinolone ring antibiotics such as ciprofloxacin: a course consists of 20 tablets and you should carry one course for each person on board. Again these drugs are only available on prescription, so you will need to consult a doctor.

Whatever activity you are enjoying, the way that your First Aid kit is packed is as important as what is in it. Make sure that you have a pack which is waterproof – otherwise when you need bandages and dressings you will find them in a sodden mass alongside a useless pair of rusty scissors.

AIDS AND HEPATATIS B

Both HIV viruses, which are associated with the development of AIDS, and the Hepatitis B virus which causes potentially fatal liver disease, are carried in the body fluids – notably blood. This means that a First Aider who comes into contact with the blood of a casualty who is infected with one of these viruses can become infected as a result of the contact. The risk is small, but nevertheless I suggest that non-sterile examination gloves should be included in the First Aid kit. They should be disposed of after one use, but they are cheap to buy and they do protect any First Aider who has to deal with wounds or any other emergency which involves handling the blood of the casualty.

	KIT 1	KIT 2	KIT 3
Micropore tape, 2.5 cm × 5 m	1	2	2
Non-stick dressings, 10 cm × 10 cm	2	10	20
Triangular bandage, 90 cm × 127 cm	2	4	4
Wound dressings, No. 8	2	4	10
Antiseptic wipes	4	10	30
Waterproof plasters (assorted sizes)	6	20	50
Elastoplast strapping, 7.5 cm rolls × 5m	1	3	6
Scissors	1	1	1
Safety pins	4	4	4
Non-sterile examination gloves (pairs)	1	5	20
Steristrips	—	1 pack	1 pack
Tubegauz finger dressing and applicator	—	1	1
Splints	—	2	2
Eyepad	—	2	2
Anthisan cream, 30 g tube	—	1	1
Calpol (for children)	—	100 ml	100 ml
Paracetamol tablets, 500 mg	—	20	100
Scopaderm TTS patches	—	4	10
Stugeron tablets, 15 mg	—	10	24
Eye drops, Predsol N 5 ml	—	—	2
Piriton tablets 4 mg	—	—	20
Non-steroidal anti-inflammatory tablets	—	—	30
Dentanurse dental kit	—	1	2

A casualty must be treated as being unconscious if he is not fully alert or cannot remain fully alert without being constantly aroused.

The main danger to an unconscious casualty is not being able to breathe – either because the jaw muscles are slack allowing the big muscles of the tongue to drop and block the air passage, or because of the inhalation of vomit.

Unconsciousness can be produced by illness, injuries, drugs or alcohol. Do not stop to decide why the casualty is unconscious. The treatment of unconsciousness by placing the casualty in the recovery position takes priority over everything other than resuscitation. Follow the steps below straight away.

> **If you have reason to believe that the casualty has a neck or back injury turn to page 42 now.**

1 Check that the casualty is breathing by watching for chest movement, and by listening for and feeling air entering and leaving the nose and/or mouth of the casualty.

2 If the casualty is not breathing or is struggling to breathe with exaggerated chest movements, lift up the lower jaw to correct jaw drop and thus lift the tongue muscles out of the way.

3 Once the jaw has been lifted check again to see if air is entering easily.

4 If the casualty is still not breathing turn to page 10 and start resuscitation immediately.

5 If after the jaw is lifted the casualty breathes check the pulse either at the wrist or in the neck.

6 If the casualty has no pulse turn to page 12 and start the complete resuscitation procedure immediately.

7 If the casualty is breathing and has a pulse place the casualty in the recovery position as follows:

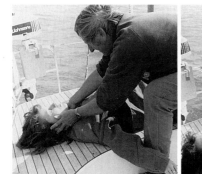

← The recovery position: first straighten her head . . .

Then place both arms by her sides . . .

And roll her towards you, onto her side.

RECOVERY POSITION

1 Kneel beside the casualty and turn his head towards you, keeping his jaw forward to keep the air passage open.

2 Place the arms of the casualty by his sides and roll him towards you so that he is on his side.

3 Pull the uppermost arm forward and bend the elbow; pull the uppermost leg forward and bend the knee.

4 The bent arm and leg will now support the casualty so that he cannot roll over onto his face or onto his back.

5 Check again to make sure that the casualty's head is in the right position to keep the air passage open.

6 Pull the lowermost arm from under the casualty, keeping it straight from the shoulder so that it lies straight alongside him. The casualty is now in the recovery position. He is stable and will not obstruct the air passage by his position. If he vomits it will run down out of his mouth and not back into his lungs.

8 Now check to see if there is any external bleeding. If there is, turn to page 16.

9 Check for any other injuries and turn to the appropriate page to deal with them, but remember that keeping the air passage clear and the casualty in a stable position has priority.

Do not leave an unconscious casualty alone. As consciousness is regained the casualty will need reassurance and maybe gentle restraint so that he does not try to move before he fully recovers his coordination.

Do not give anything by mouth to anyone who is not fully alert or he may choke and die.

If the casualty remains unconscious you will need to move him to a warm, dry, safe place where he can remain in the recovery position. Turn to page 86 for instructions on how to move the casualty.

Use the section on *Communications* (page 82) to get advice and medical help. Anyone who has been unconscious should be examined by a doctor as soon as possible.

Make sure her jaw is held up and forward so that the airway is clear.

Pull the top arm forward and bend the elbow, then pull the top leg forward and bend the knee . . .

And extend the lower arm down by her side.

After a serious accident or sudden illness the two vital life support functions of the body may cease to function. These two functions are: breathing to take in oxygen from the air, and heartbeat to take the oxygen in the blood to all parts of the body. If one or both of these systems fails no oxygen will reach the brain and the casualty will soon die.

Artificial ventilation is used to replace breathing and external cardiac compression is used to replace natural heartbeat. If these resuscitation methods are properly performed normal breathing and heartbeat may resume and the casualty should revive.

ARTIFICIAL VENTILATION

Use the mouth-to-mouth method of artificial ventilation, as follows:

1   Is the casualty breathing? If the chest is moving rhythmically and you can feel and/or hear air going in and out of the casualty's mouth or nose you have no need to perform artificial ventilation. If the chest is moving violently but there is no air passing through the nose and mouth then the airway is obstructed, so continue as described in paragraph 2 below. If there is no chest movement and there is no movement of air through the mouth and nose, go to paragraph 2 below.

2   The most important part of resuscitation is to make sure that the air passages of the casualty are not obstructed. Open the mouth and with your finger remove any vomit, sweets or chewing gum. Remove false teeth if they are loose, but if they are firm leave them.

3   With the casualty lying on his back kneel by his right shoulder. With your right hand lift the lower jaw and push it forwards, and at the same time place your left hand on the brow of the casualty and tilt the head backwards; this automatically lifts the tongue and stops it blocking the air passage. (If this is difficult because of obstructions nearby, kneel at his left side and reverse the hand positions.)

4   Watch to see if the casualty's chest now moves rhythmically and listen for air entering and leaving. If this happens you have opened up the airway and the casualty can now breathe normally. If the casualty is not fully conscious place him in the recovery position and continue to support his jaw to keep open the airway. If his chest does not move and you can sense no air movement do not put the patient into the recovery position but carry on to artificial ventilation.

◆ Artificial ventilation: lie the casualty on her back . . .

And remove anything from her mouth that might be blocking her airway.

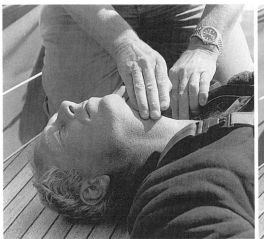
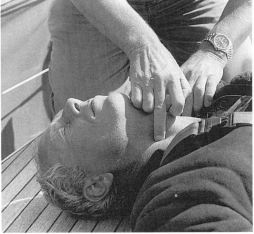

5 Remove your left hand from his brow and pinch his nostrils together to close off the nose. Keeping your right hand under the raised lower jaw place your mouth over the mouth of the casualty and blow air firmly into him. If the position is correct you will see his chest rise and fall and you will hear the air come out again.

6 After you have performed five satisfactory inflations of the chest at roughly six-second intervals check the casualty's pulse to see that there is a heartbeat. Check in the neck to feel for the pulse in the carotid artery: place two

← To find the pulse in the carotid artery place two fingers on the Adam's apple (left), slide them down the side and press into the muscle towards the spine. If all is well you should feel the pulse easily.

fingers on the Adam's apple, slide your fingers down the side of the Adam's apple until you feel the muscle, then press backwards and inwards towards the spine to feel the pulse. If there *is* a pulse continue artificial ventilation 12 times per minute and check the pulse every three minutes. If there is no carotid pulse start external cardiac compression straight away. Turn to the next page.

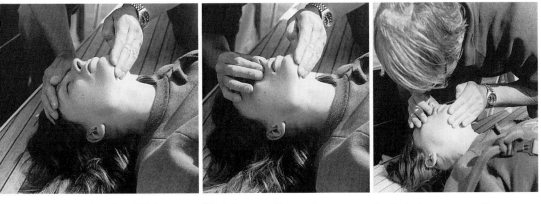

Tilt her head back and lift her jaw upward and forward to lift the tongue clear of the airway.

Pinch her nostrils together while holding her jaw up . . .

And, placing your mouth over hers, blow air firmly into her.

  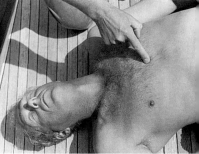

← The top of the breastbone is in the V of the collarbone just below the Adam's apple.

The bottom of the breastbone is in the V of the ribs above the stomach.

The compression point is one third of the way up the breastbone from its bottom end.

External cardiac compression is the technique used to replace the natural heartbeat when the heart is failing to maintain circulation of the blood. When you compress the heart it acts as a simple mechanical pump, and its valves make sure that the blood flows in the right direction.

← If you are on your own you should alternate 12 cycles of cardiac compression (left) with two cycles of mouth-to-mouth ventilation (right).

Procedure

1 With the casualty lying flat on his back identify the breastbone (sternum). This bone runs down the centre of the front of the chest from the neck to the upper abdomen.

2 Kneel beside the casualty facing his chest and place the heel of your right hand in the centre of the casualty's chest on the lower third of the breastbone. Place your left hand on top of your right hand.

Place the heel of your right hand on the compression point over the casualty's heart.

Put your left hand on top of your right hand and lock your arms stiff and straight. You are now ready to begin cardiac compression.

3 Rock forward with your arms locked straight and stiff so that your weight presses down on the breastbone. You will feel it move downwards with the force. The bone should move approximately 4 cm (1½ in). Rock back so that your weight is off the casualty and the breastbone will spring upwards.

4 Repeat this cycle every second.

5 Pause after every fifth cycle so that another First Aider can peform one cycle of mouth-to-mouth ventilation. If you are on your own, perform 12 cycles of cardiac compression, then two cycles of mouth-to-mouth.

6 Continue until you are sure that the casualty has a pulse in the neck and remains pink after you stop cardiac compression.

7 Stop mouth-to-mouth artificial ventilation only when the casualty is breathing regularly on his own.

☛ If there are two First Aiders available, alternate five cycles of cardiac compression with one cycle of mouth-to-mouth ventilation. Do not try to perform both at the same time.

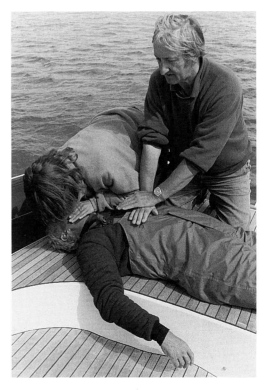

The safest and surest way of stopping bleeding is by direct pressure on the site of the bleeding. In the very rare event of severe injury to a limb involving the opening of major arteries when direct pressure will not stop the bleeding, see opposite under *Tourniquet*.

> **Remember: in cases where there is blood loss always put on a pair of gloves from the First Aid kit before starting to deal with the casualty.**

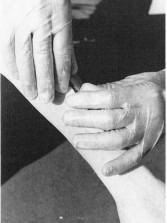 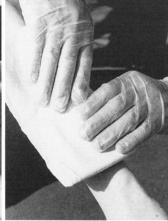 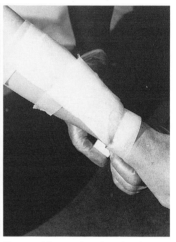

◄ Hold the edges of the wound together and apply direct pressure to stop the bleeding.

Cover the wound with a clean dressing, but keep up the pressure.

Cover with a pad and maintain the pressure while you apply an elastic adhesive bandage.

Direct pressure

1   Hold the edges of the wound together and apply pressure to the wound with your fingers.

2   Place a clean dressing over the wound, then press directly onto the dressing.

3   Cover the dressing with a pad. If the bleeding continues add more padding, but do not disturb the first dressing. Continue to apply pressure to the pad.

4   Apply an elastic adhesive bandage tightly over the pad. If the bleeding is from a limb continue the elastic bandage right round the limb, then check the casualty's fingers and toes to make sure that the circulation has not been completely stopped. The fingers and toes must remain pink after the bandage is applied, and not become white or blue. If they do become white or blue take off the bandage and reapply it less tightly.

◄ After bandaging a limb check the fingers or toes. If they turn white or blue the bandage is too tight.

5   Once the bleeding has stopped turn to *Wounds* (page 34) to find out how to deal with the wound and whether or not to seek medical aid urgently.

USING A TOURNIQUET TO STOP BLEEDING

> **A tourniquet should only be used in cases of very severe injury when direct pressure will not stop the bleeding and there is a threat to life from blood loss.**

1 Wrap a piece of rope around the injured limb immediately above the injury. Tie a knot in the rope.

2 Place a strong bar of wood or metal about 30 cm (12 in) long on the knot, then tie another knot in the rope over the bar.

3 Twist the bar so as to tighten the rope around the limb. Keep twisting and tightening until the bleeding stops.

4 Once applied, the tourniquet must be loosened every 20 minutes to allow oxygen to pass to the remainder of the limb. If the bleeding starts again when the tourniquet is loosened, re-tighten it and release it again after a further 20 minutes. If there is no bleeding after loosening the tourniquet leave it loose – but watch the wound in case heavy bleeding re-starts.

5 Turn to page 34 and read the section on *Wounds*.

> **Any casualty who has had an injury severe enough to warrant the application of a tourniquet needs to receive medical attention with the utmost urgency.**

For a tourniquet, wrap a rope around the limb just above the injury and tie a reef knot.

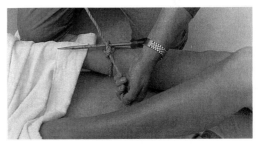

Place a bar over the knot and tie another reef knot above it.

Twist the bar to tighten the rope, compress the blood vessels and stop the bleeding.

Loosen the tourniquet every 20 minutes to allow blood to flow to the rest of the limb.

External bleeding from some sites can be difficult to deal with, but direct pressure will stop the bleeding if you apply it correctly.

Remember: in cases of blood loss always put on a pair of gloves from the First Aid kit before starting to deal with the casualty.

BLEEDING FROM THE NOSE

Bleeding from the small veins on the inside of the nose is a common and troublesome problem.

1   Simply hold the fleshy, soft part of the nose between your forefinger and thumb firmly but not painfully. Maintain the pressure for 15 minutes.

2   After 15 minutes release your grip; if the bleeding starts again when you have let go, hold the nose for a further 15 minutes.

BLEEDING FROM THE PALM OF THE HAND

1   Place a clean dressing on the wound and press directly on it for 20 minutes.

2   Release the pressure and make sure the bleeding has stopped. Ask the casualty to make a fist around the pad, then bandage firmly around the close fist with an elastic adhesive bandage.

➤ Applying a dressing to the palm of the hand.

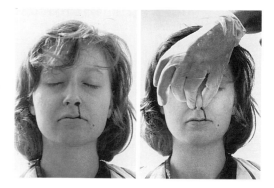

➤ To stop a nosebleed, simply squeeze the nostrils for 15 minutes. Note the gloves.

BLEEDING FROM THE SCALP

The scalp is very well supplied with small blood vessels and even small wounds of the scalp bleed heavily. There is no way of bandaging the scalp to exert enough pressure to stop bleeding, so you have to apply the pressure yourself over a relatively long period.

1   Apply firm direct pressure onto a pad over a clean dressing for at least 30 minutes. Check to see that the bleeding has stopped. If not, apply pressure to the pad for another 30 minutes.

2   When the bleeding has stopped cover the wound with a clean dressing and tape it on.

3   Unless the wound on the scalp is a minor scratch remember to check for other head injuries such as fracture of the skull or

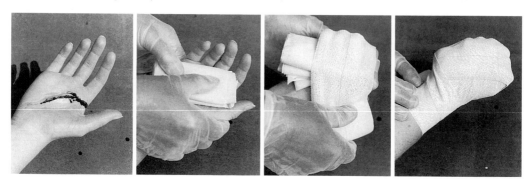

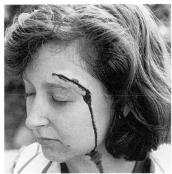

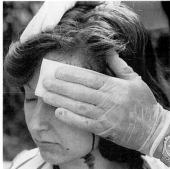

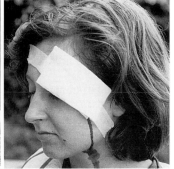

← A scalp wound will bleed heavily, even if it is quite superficial.

Stop it by applying pressure to a pad over a clean dressing for at least 30 minutes.

When the bleeding has stopped apply a clean dressing and pad, and tape them on.

concussion. Turn to page 28 to check the level of response. Remember that concussion may not be apparent until some time after the injury, so keep the casualty in a safe place and check his response level after 20 minutes.

BLEEDING FROM A TOOTH SOCKET

1 Wash out the mouth with warm water, and remove any blood clot from the bleeding socket.

2 Roll up a pad of clean dressing and place it in the socket. Tell the casualty to bite firmly on the pad for 20 minutes.

3 Remove the pad, and repeat if the bleeding restarts.

BLEEDING FROM A VARICOSE VEIN IN THE LEG

1 Lie the casualty down, then raise the bleeding leg by resting the heel on a berth or table.

2 Apply a clean dressing to the bleeding point, then a pad. Fasten firmly with an elastic adhesive bandage around the leg.

♦ Treat a bleeding varicose vein by raising the leg, applying a dressing and bandaging firmly.

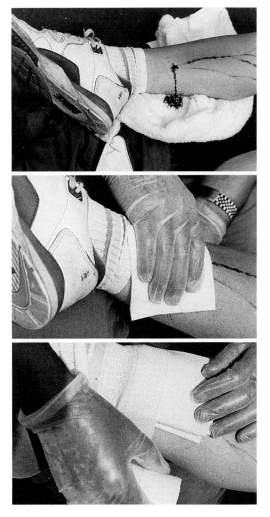

Water drawn into the air passages will stop oxygen getting through the lungs and into the bloodstream. The first organs to be critically affected by the resulting lack of oxygen in their blood supply are the brain and the heart.

The aim is to get air into the lungs and, if necessary, pump the oxygenated blood to the tissues.

> **Danger: Only go into the water to a drowning person if it is safe for you to do so.**

As soon as possible – but without endangering yourself – start mouth-to-mouth ventilation. Do not wait to make sure that the casualty is not breathing. If he *is* breathing he will resist your efforts and be none the worse for them. So:

1 Clear any loose matter from the mouth, then pull up the lower jaw of the casualty and tilt his head back to make sure that the air passage is clear.

2 Holding up his jaw with one hand, pinch his nose between the forefinger and thumb of your other hand to close it off, then breathe into his mouth. When you have put five good breaths into his lungs stop for a moment to assess the situation.

3 Should you get the casualty to a safer place? If you should, make a plan to do so but give another five ventilations before you do it. If you are in a safe position continue to resuscitate.

4 Feel for the pulse in the casualty's neck to see if he has a heartbeat. Place your fingers on the casualty's Adam's apple, then slide them down to the muscle running down the front of the neck. Push firmly backwards and inwards towards the spine and feel for the pulse. If he has a pulse but is not breathing for himself, continue mouth-to-mouth ventilation. If he has no pulse start external cardiac compression as well.

5 With the casualty lying flat on his back identify the breastbone (sternum). This bone runs down the centre of the front of the chest from the neck to the upper abdomen.

6 Kneel beside the casualty facing his chest and place the heel of your right hand in the centre of the casualty's chest on the lower third of the breastbone. Place your left hand on top of your right hand.

7 Rock forward with your arms locked straight and stiff so that your weight presses down on the breastbone. You will feel it move downwards with the force. The bone should move approximately 4 cm (1½ in). Rock back

Getting someone out of the water is hard work. Here a lifeboat crew heave him up . . .

Push him down against the forces of buoyancy . . .

And heave him up again as he pops up like a cork.

 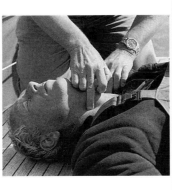 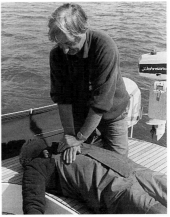

☛ The first priority is five cycles of mouth-to-mouth ventilation.

☛ Then feel for the pulse in the casualty's neck.

☛ If there is no pulse, start external cardiac compression, alternating with ventilation.

so that your weight is off the casualty, and the breastbone will spring upwards.

8 Repeat this cycle every second.

9 Pause after every fifth cycle so that another First Aider can perform one cycle of mouth-to-mouth. If you are on your own perform 12 cycles of cardiac compression, then two cycles of mouth-to-mouth.

10 Continue until you are sure that the casualty has a pulse in the neck and remains pink after you stop cardiac compression.

11 Stop mouth-to-mouth ventilation only when the casualty is breathing regularly unaided.

When the casualty has a steady pulse and is breathing normally, check him over for other injuries. Bear in mind that many people who have been immersed in water will be suffering from hypothermia (lowered body temperature). Turn to page 22 for the treatment of hypothermia.

Any casualty who has been resuscitated after being immersed in water must be taken for medical assessment as soon as possible.

They pull him clear of the water. . . Into the boat . . .

And start mouth-to-mouth ventilation immediately.

The human body is normally kept within very narrow limits of temperature. There are mechanisms to prevent us getting too hot, and we produce heat in various ways to compensate for heat loss. But if the body loses heat very quickly it may not be able to produce heat fast enough to replace the loss: its temperature drops and the result is hypothermia.

Water is a good conductor, so anyone who is wet through or immersed in water loses heat quickly and soon becomes hypothermic. Wind also causes rapid heat loss.

Crew who get their clothing wet through, especially if they are exposed to wind on deck, will very quickly become hypothermic. Anybody immersed in the sea when the sea temperature is less than 10°C (50°F) will become hypothermic within two or three hours.

The effects of hypothermia range in severity from feeling cold and shivering to being unconscious and apparently dead.

Treatment

1 Your first aim is to prevent further heat loss. Get the casualty out of the sea and out of the wind.

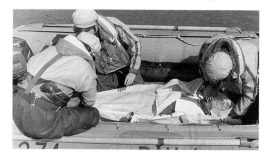

← Lifeboats carry thermal bags that can be zipped around a hypothermic casualty to prevent further heat loss.

2 If the casualty is on board but wet through, get him into the warmest spot on board and turn on all heating. As soon as possible strip off all wet clothing, by cutting it off if necessary. Do not rub the skin to dry it but simply dab it dry with a towel.

3 If the casualty is conscious get him into warm dry clothing, give him lots of warm sweet drinks and allow him to rest in a warm sheltered spot. If you are dinghy sailing or canoeing get the casualty safely ashore, find shelter and provide warmth. If you have no other means of providing warmth get close enough to transfer your body heat to the casualty.

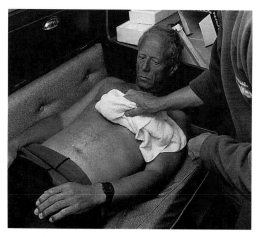

← Remove wet clothing and dab the casualty dry with a towel. Do not rub, since this causes heat loss.

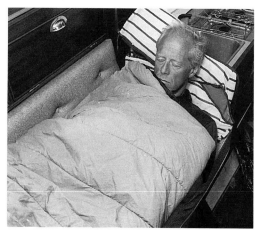

← Wrap him up well and turn on some form of heating – in this case the galley cooker.

4 If the casualty is unconscious or too cold to help himself take off all his wet clothing and put him into a sleeping bag. Make sure that there is no draught and that the area around the casualty is made as warm as possible. If you have no heaters light the gas cooker.

5 If the boat is cold and it will take time to warm it up, get into the sleeping bag with the casualty. You should wear light clothing to speed up the transfer of the heat. If the casualty is not fully alert make sure that he is in the recovery position in the sleeping bag and that he is in no danger of suffocating.

Someone who becomes very cold over a period of time will go into a state of semi-hibernation, so although he does not seem to be breathing adequately and has a weak or absent pulse the fact that he is so cold means that the oxygen requirements of his body are greatly reduced. So if the casualty is pulled from the sea cold and apparently dead you should try to resuscitate him. Turn to page 12 and go through the resuscitation procedures. At the same time you must stop the casualty losing any more heat and gradually warm him up. You should only stop resuscitation procedures if there is no response to treatment when the casualty is back to normal temperature.

FROSTBITE

Frostbite is cold injury to a localised area of skin and underlying tissue. It varies in severity from a small area of white waxy skin (frost nip) to blistered blue or black areas where all the tissue is frozen and dead.

However superficial frostbite seems to be it must be treated seriously or permanent injury may follow.

Treatment
1 Warm the affected area with any sort of heat except a naked flame. One way is to immerse it in water that is pleasantly warm to the touch, at about 42°C (110°F).

2 When the injured area is warmed make sure that it is rested and is padded and bandaged to prevent damage. If the casualty has frostbite of the feet walking and standing must be limited to the absolute minimum necessary. Get him to lie down with his feet raised on a well-padded footrest. If there is frostbite of the fingers or hand pad the damaged part and place the arm in a full arm sling.

3 Give the casualty plenty of warm food and drinks, and make sure he rests.

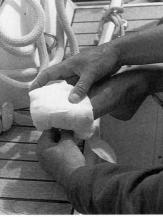
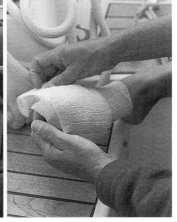

➤ Frostbite: warm the area and carefully apply a dressing

Apply a pad to cushion the injury against further shock . . .

And wrap it in several layers of crepe bandage.

Seasickness is both unpleasant and potentially dangerous since it reduces the number of crew who are able to perform routine tasks on board. What's more, the sight of someone suffering from seasickness along with the smell of vomit can soon cause others to become ill.

The first signs of seasickness are lassitude followed by nausea which quickly develops to actual vomiting. The symptoms are seldom relieved by vomiting and the casualty becomes unsteady, faint and has to lie down with his eyes closed.

Prevention
- Avoid a hangover on the day that you sail. Eve-of-race parties are part of the boating scene but are a major cause of seasickness.
- Watch what you eat. Choose bland foods that are quickly absorbed, both on the day before you go to sea and on the morning itself. Have biscuits and sweets handy on board so that if you don't feel like a meal you can top up your blood sugar. Glucose tablets and bananas are good. Drink plenty of non-alcoholic, non-fizzy drinks.
- Keep warm; wear plenty of protective waterproof clothing.
- Wear a Scopaderm TTS patch for at least eight hours before you are going to go aboard.

Advice for skippers
Fear and anxiety play a part in seasickness, so you should go to sea in a quietly confident manner and tell your crew what your plans are. If any of the crew have anxieties, discuss them to show that you are aware of them and have contingency plans. Do not shout at crew members or blame them for cock-ups; that sort of behaviour is merely a manifestation of your lack of confidence in yourself.

Make sure that each crew member is asked to do things that he is capable of doing. Keep an eye on them all, and if you think that someone is feeling seedy let him stay on deck (in shelter as far as possible) and cheer him up.

Keep your boat clean and sweet-smelling.

◆ Don't let a seasickness victim follow her breakfast over the side! Clip her into the cockpit and give her a bucket.

Treatment
1   If somebody is feeling queasy make sure that he is warmly clothed. Allow him to stay on deck if he wishes to but make sure he is clipped on by lifeline. Give him a bucket if he is going to throw up, but don't let him onto the side deck: an unsteady seasickness sufferer is all too likely to disappear over the side, all in the cause of gentility.

2   If the seasickness progresses to actual vomiting and the casualty is unable to carry on with normal tasks get him below, allow him to rest or, better still, sleep – but make sure there's a bucket to hand.

3   Remember that seasickness sufferers become extremely unsteady and faint, so put the casualty in the securest place and make sure that he does not need to move. Reassure him.

4   Stay calm. People with seasickness feel and look terrible. They sometimes bring up a little blood from dry retching and they may

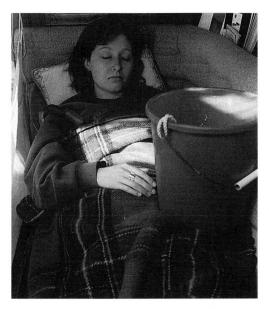

← Lying full-length on a bunk will often relieve seasickness, but make sure there's a bucket within easy reach.

give you grave cause for concern. But do not be tempted into putting the boat at risk to get someone with seasickness ashore to medical aid. I have seen men who have been totally prostrate with seasickness for days jump ashore and run from the boat as soon as they know that land is at hand. Recovery is miraculous once they set foot on terra firma.

DRUGS USED FOR SEASICKNESS PREVENTION

Many of the drugs used to reduce nausea have sedative effects and are therefore unsuitable for people who are going to sea and need to be alert and nimble.

Cinnarizine, sold also as Stugeron, is widely used although it does produce sedation in some people. It should be taken from at least four hours before going on board in a dose of 15 mg every eight hours. It is of course no good giving drugs by mouth once the casualty is being sick.

An alternative to tablets is to apply a plaster impregnated with hyoscine so that the drug is absorbed through the skin. This preparation is known as Scopaderm TTS and it is available only on prescription from a doctor. Although best applied well before going on board it is worth applying if someone becomes sick.

Bracelets which put pressure on the forearm just above the wrist have been shown to be effective; they are sold as Sea Bands.

← The Scopaderm TTS patch is best applied to the skin just behind the ear. Be sure to wash your hands afterwards, because the preparation can have alarming effects on your eyes.

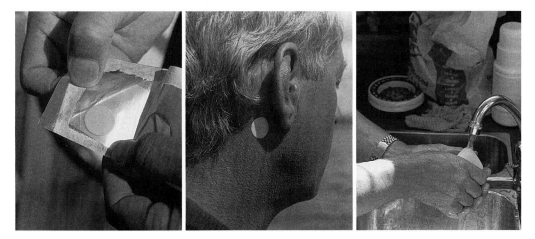

HEAT EXHAUSTION AND HEAT STROKE

The body makes heat during exercise and may take in heat from the environment. It loses heat by convection, conduction, through breathing and particularly by sweating. When the body produces more heat than it can lose its temperature begins to rise until, eventually, its temperature regulation systems fail altogether. The body also suffers a deficiency of water and possibly salt.

Heat exhaustion occurs when the casualty's temperature is moderately raised to over 39°C: he is thirsty, restless, sweats profusely, feels sick, has a headache, becomes unsteady and may behave oddly. Heatstroke occurs when the body loses control of temperature regulation and its temperature rises to 42°C or above.

Treatment: heat exhaustion

1 Rest the casualty in the shade.

2 Cool him by wrapping his body in a sheet soaked in cold water. Pour more cold water on the sheet from time to time.

3 Give him large quantities of water by mouth: two litres in the first hour, then one litre per hour until he is passing plenty of clear urine. Add one level teaspoonful of salt to each litre of water.

← Wrap a heatstroke victim in a sheet soaked in cold water, and add more cold water at intervals. If possible, do this in a shaded place.

Heatstroke

Treatment is as for heat exhaustion but the cooling process must be carried out quickly and remorselessly. If the casualty is unconscious place him in the recovery position (see page 10) and do not give drinks by mouth.

SUNBURN

Sunburn is caused by ultra-violet radiation from the sun. The clear, clean air at sea does not filter out the ultra-violet radiation as much as the hazy air over land, so more gets through and can burn. If there is a breeze at sea you may stay cool but there is no reduction in the amount of ultra-violet radiation; as a result you may become burned without noticing until it is too late. Reflection from the surface of calm water or even from a white sail can increase the amount of ultra-violet radiation that hits your skin.

Prevention
Avoid sunburn by wearing protective clothing, staying in the shade or by using an effective ultra-violet blocking cream.

Treatment
1   Do not burst blisters.

2   Place the casualty in the shade and give him frequent watery drinks.

3   Apply calamine or an anti-histamine cream such as Anthisan.

4   If the skin is very sore give two paracetamol tablets every 4–6 hours.

DEHYDRATION

Water balance is important. If someone takes in excess fluid his kidneys will excrete the excess, but if he does not take in fluid or loses a great deal through sweating or diarrhoea the kidneys still excrete some water and he still loses some through breathing. If he takes in less water than he excretes he will eventually become dehydrated. This happens quickly if the casualty has severe diarrhoea, or a fever that causes profuse sweating.

Treatment
1   The casualty will be deficient in salt and minerals as well as water so, rather than give plain water, make up the following fluid:
- 1 litre of boiled water
- 20 g glucose (1.5 teaspoons honey or sugar)
- 3.5 g salt (½ teaspoonful table salt)
- 2.5 g sodium bicarbonate (½ teaspoonful baking soda)
- 1.5 g potassium chloride (2 cups fruit juice)

2   If possible give large quantities of this fluid by mouth at a rate of 1–2 litres per hour until the casualty passes lots of clear urine.

3   If the casualty is nauseated or vomiting and cannot drink, the fluid may be administered through the rectum. Pass a greased tube about 1 cm (½ in) diameter through the anus and for another 15 cm (6 in) into the rectum, then pour the fluid in through the tube. This is an unpleasant business but if you are several days from help with a seriously ill casualty it can speed recovery and may even save a life.

Injury to the head can cause several types of problem: unconsciousness, scalp wounds, even a fractured skull.

If the casualty has been knocked unconscious, turn to page 10 immediately.

A wound on the scalp is likely to bleed profusely, because the scalp is very well supplied with blood vessels. Turn to page 18 for the treatment of bleeding, either from the scalp, from the nose or from a tooth socket. Turn to page 34 for the treatment of wounds.

If you can see that the casualty has a fractured skull, turn to page 40. If there is no obvious fracture or crushing, read on.

Initial care and observation
If the casualty has had a bang on the head but does not seem to have any of the conditions mentioned above, this does not mean that he is uninjured. The skull surrounds and protects the brain, but the force of any blow to the

➡ Someone with a head injury will be unsteady and in danger of falling overboard, so support her and help her below to a safe place.

outside of the skull is transmitted through the bone to the brain. This means that the brain may be bruised, or there may be blood loss into the brain without any sign of damage to the outside of the head.

After a blow to the head the casualty may feel dizzy and be unsteady. This is obviously dangerous on any vessel since the casualty may fall overboard, so make sure that anyone who has had a bang on the head goes below to a secure place where you can observe him. He should rest, and you should check his responsiveness every quarter of an hour for the first two hours and then, if the level remains satisfactory, every hour. Check the level of responsiveness like this:

1 Talk to the casualty. You will get information in two ways. Ask if he has a headache, does he feel giddy, has he been sick or does he feel sick? If the answer to any of these questions is "yes" the head injury has had some ill-effects. The way the casualty answers these questions will also tell you something. Is his speech normal and does he answer the questions promptly? Is his speech confused or does he take longer than normal to answer? Are his answers appropriate, inappropriate, merely noises or is there no response at all?

2 Look at his eyes. Are they open and focused, do they open only when you speak to him or are they closed all the time?

3 Does the casualty move when and how you ask him to? Can he perform simple tasks with his hands such as finding a page in the nautical almanac?

4 Can he remember the accident and the period immediately before and after it?

From these simple tests you can get a good idea of the casualty's level of consciousness. More importantly you can repeat the examination every quarter-hour to find out if the level is steady, getting better or getting worse.

▲ Checking response levels: first talk to the casualty.

Look at her eyes – are they open and focused?

Ask her to do some simple task – does she get confused?

If the level is steady or getting better you can plan how and when you will get the casualty ashore, or you may decide that there is no need to interrupt your passage.

If the response level is getting worse, you must make every effort to get the casualty ashore to medical attention. Meanwhile you must get him into a secure place where you can place him in the recovery position (see page 10).

➡ If the casualty becomes unconscious place her in the recovery position and get her to medical aid as soon as possible.

If he becomes more nauseated as time goes on, or is sick more than once, or the level of response becomes lower, you must get him to medical aid as quickly as possible. Alert the emergency services and ask for help.

> **Remember that anybody who has been unconscious must go to hospital for observation.**

Injuries to the chest are potentially dangerous because they may involve the heart or lungs.

PENETRATING INJURIES TO THE CHEST

1 If you suspect that the casualty has sustained an injury to the chest get him into shelter as quickly as possible and strip him to the waist. As well as looking for bleeding, examine him carefully to see if air is being sucked in or blown out of any wounds as he breathes. Listen for the air going in or out.

2 If there is such a wound cover it with an airtight dressing: three layers of melolin dressing covered with a piece of plastic sheet and fastened to the chest wall with layers of adhesive elastic bandage.

3 Settle the casualty as comfortably as possible. If he is conscious do not insist that he lies flat; allow him to sit up in the position that allows him to breathe easily.

4 Let him rest, reassure him and give two paracetamol tablets every four hours if he is in pain.

← Quickly strip the casualty to the waist, cutting his clothes off if necessary.

5 Anybody with a penetrating chest wound needs urgent hospitalisation, so you should either head for shore or call for assistance (see page 82).

6 If the casualty becomes unconscious before you can get him to hospital place him in the recovery position (page 10), making sure that the good side of his chest (away from the injury) is uppermost.

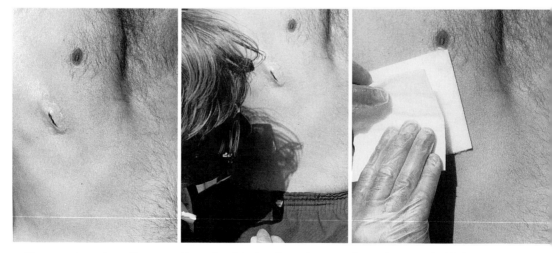

← The wound may be quite small, but it could be deep and potentially very dangerous.

Listen for air being drawn in and out of the wound – one sign of a penetrating injury.

Cover the wound with three layers of dressing and a piece of plastic sheet . . .

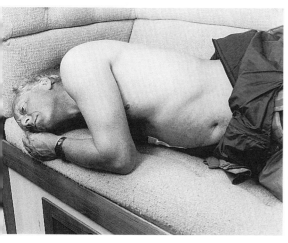

← If the casualty falls unconscious put him in the recovery position, lying on his injured side.

CRUSH INJURIES TO THE CHEST

If there is no wound but the chest is crushed treat as above without applying a dressing.

See also page 44 for treatment of fractured ribs.

← If the casualty is fully conscious allow him to sit in any position that allows him to breathe easily, but make sure he is secure.

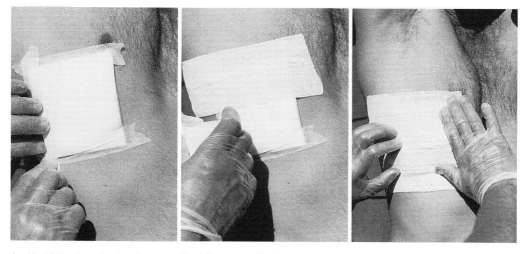

And hold the dressing in place with adhesive tape.

Seal the area with plenty of adhesive elastic bandage . . .

And make sure the whole thing is airtight.

Choking is caused by a foreign body blocking the air passage so that the casualty cannot breathe.

The casualty will be silent, his lips will become blue and he may clutch at his throat. Eventually he will become unconscious if the obstruction is not removed.

Treatment

1 Look into his mouth. If you can see the foreign body and you are sure that you can remove it with your fingers without risk of pushing it more firmly into the air passage, carefully remove it.

2 If you cannot see the foreign body, or you are afraid that you may push it further in, use blows on the back. Support the casualty's breastbone with one hand, and give four sharp, rapid blows with the heel of your hand between the shoulder blades.

3 Open his mouth and remove the foreign body if it is now free.

4 If this treatment fails you will need to use abdominal thrusts. Stand behind the patient, place one clenched fist in the centre of his upper abdomen, grasp the fist with your other hand and give four sharp thrusts inwards and upwards. This will force air out of the lungs strongly enough to dislodge the obstruction.

← If someone is choking, support her breastbone or, as here, lean her forward against her knees before slapping her four times between the shoulder blades to eject the obstacle.

← Abdominal thrusts: place one clenched fist on the upper abdomen (left), hold this in the other hand (right) and give four sharp thrusts inward and upward. With a child, use just one hand.

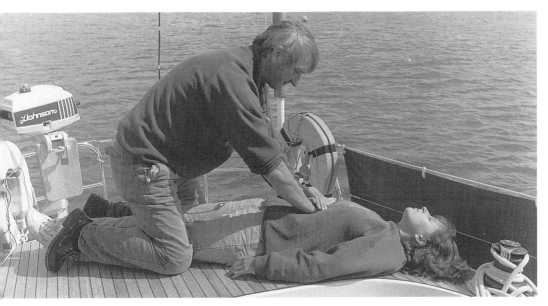

⬥ You can use the abdominal thrust technique on an unconscious casualty lying on her back.

If the casualty is unconscious

1   Lie the casualty on his back.

2   Kneel astride him.

3   Place your hands in the centre of the casualty's upper abdomen just below the ribs.

4   Push upwards and inwards.

5   Repeat five times if necessary.

⬥ It may be easier to slap the casualty's back if she lies down, but support her breastbone.

CHILDREN CHOKING

Small children and infants are so small that the usual techniques need to be adapted to suit them.

1   Be very, very careful about trying to remove the obstruction with your finger. It is very easy to push the foreign body further into the air passage of a small child and cause a complete obstruction which is impossible to remove.

2   Kneel on one knee, hold the child face-down over your other knee and, supporting the child's chest with one hand, tap him firmly between the shoulder blades.

3   If that does not dislodge the obstruction place the child in front of you facing away from you, place your clenched fist on the upper abdomen, and with just the one hand give a sharp upward and inward push.

Small infants

Lie the child on his back with the air passage held open by the jaw, then with two fingers give a sharp upward and inward push into the upper abdomen.

Wounds are breaks in the skin or mucous membranes, which may be caused in several ways by different kinds of trauma. The resulting gap in the body's defences causes external bleeding which must be stopped first of all. Turn to page 16 for the methods of stopping bleeding.

Once you have dealt with the bleeding you should treat the wound itself to prevent complications such as scarring and infection. Where medical help is readily available a simple clean dressing over the wound is all that is required until the casualty is in medical care an hour or two later. But if you are on a long offshore or ocean passage you will need to do more to protect the wound for several days.

Always wear a pair of examination gloves if you are likely to come into contact with blood, since they will protect you against viral infection.

Treatment

1 Clean the wound. This is essential to prevent infection of the wound which will affect the surrounding tissues and even spread to the rest of the body. Use plenty of warm water with a disinfectant in it. Although it is painful, the wound must be cleaned thoroughly so that all loose particles are removed.

2 If it is impossible to remove all the debris from a jagged wound, and it still looks dirty after you have done your best to clean it, do not try to close it. Leave the wound as it is with a dressing over it. Change the dressing every day until you get to medical aid.

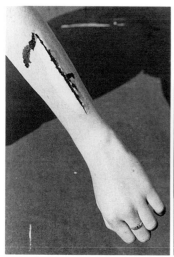

← Clean the wound thoroughly with warm water and a little disinfectant. Try to remove all foreign matter.

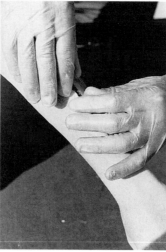

Draw the edges of the wound together with your fingers to close the gash.

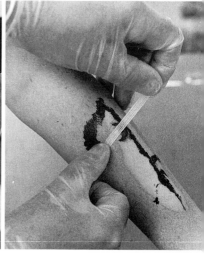

Hold the edges of the wound together with a series of butterfly sutures, leaving some space between them.

3 In most cases you will be able to get the wound clean enough for it to be closed.
To close the wound draw the edges together with your fingers and put butterfly sutures (Steristrips) across the wound to hold the edges together. If the wound is irregular it may be difficult to get the edges exactly together but it is still worth pulling them as close as possible before applying the sutures. This is a surprisingly successful method of treating wounds; many wounds which years ago would have been treated with stitches are now dealt with in this less traumatic way.

4 After you have applied the butterfly sutures cover the wound with a clean dressing and leave it until you can get medical attention.

5 If the wound is on the arm put the arm in a full arm sling (page 46).

6 If the wound is on the leg rest the casualty lying down with the injured leg raised.

7 If you are on a long ocean passage leave the dressing if the wound is comfortable. But if there is redness spreading up the limb, or if the wound is painful when the casualty is at rest, remove the dressing to see if there is infection and inflammation.

8 If there is inflammation the skin around the wound will be reddened and tender and there will be white, yellowish, green or even brownish pus weeping from the wound itself. Any wound in this condition requires urgent medical attention, and you should seek medical aid as soon as possible. If you are on an ocean passage and carrying antibiotics, use them in the dosage recommended.

Note Any wound to the chest or abdomen must be regarded as serious since it is easy for a sharp instrument to penetrate the skin and muscles and injure the internal organs. Even a small stab wound of the abdomen or chest which does not gape and hardly bleeds may have allowed a long thin instrument to penetrate far enough to rupture a lung, bowel or bladder. If a casualty has a penetrating wound of the chest or abdomen, however trivial it may be at the surface, he needs thorough examination and observation in hospital.

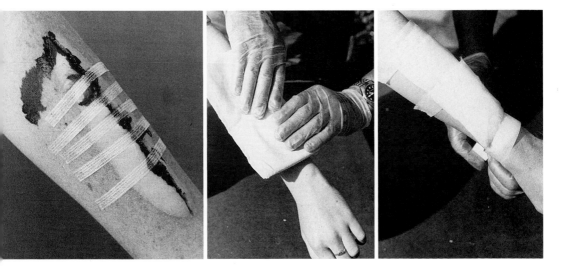

The sutures hold the wound together as effectively as stitches, and will not scar.

Cover the sutured wound with a clean dressing . . .

And hold it in place with elastic adhesive bandage.

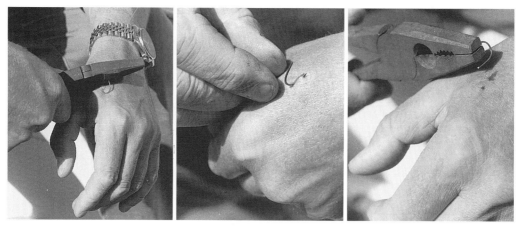

◄ To remove a fish hook, first cut off the eye (and line).

Then push the barbed point out through the skin . . .

Then grip the point in the pliers and pull the shaft out.

FISH HOOK IN THE SKIN

A fish hook embedded in the skin is difficult to remove because it has a barb which prevents it being pulled out. So if the barb is in the skin the eye of the hook and the line attached to it must be cut off.

The remains of the hook can then be pushed forward so that the barbed point emerges through another break in the skin, allowing you to pull it out from the point. The best surgical instrument for this manoeuvre is a good pair of pliers.

BRUISES

Bruises are wounds that involve loss of blood into the tissues but not through the skin. A bruise usually appears as a dark discolouration under the skin and changes colour as the blood is broken down and absorbed.

Treatment

Place the limb in a comfortable position with support and rest it. Examine the limb to see if there are signs of a fracture. If so, turn to pages 46–53.

BRUISE UNDER A FINGERNAIL

A blow to a fingernail causes a small bruise to form under the nail which is seen as a reddish-purple discolouration. Because the bruise is under pressure it is extremely painful.

Take a thin wire – an opened-up paperclip is ideal – and heat it until it glows. Use this to burn a hole through the fingernail over the bruise. It will take several heatings of the clip to burn right through. There will be a spurt of blood through the hole and the relief from pain is instantaneous.

SUPERGLUE

Histoacril (a new superglue) can be used to glue together the skin edges in clean, superficial cuts. This method can be a great benefit to long distance sailors as it is more secure than butterfly sutures and does not require suturing (stitching) with a needle. Clean the wound, squeeze the glue into the open wound and then hold the edges together for 30 seconds. Finally dress the wound as usual. Histoacril is available from Davis & Geck, Cyanamid House, Gosport or your local hospital supplier.

Although the average boat has a 12-volt system there are plenty of opportunities to get a high-voltage electric shock. Many marinas offer mains connection facilities, and when working on the boat you may use power tools supplied with 240 volts from the mains or a generator. Some navigational instruments such as radar can produce a high voltage even after being switched off – and you may even be struck by lightning! The treatment given below is appropriate for any of these.

The effects of electric shock are multiple; surface burns where the current enters the body or where it exits to earth, internal injuries, fractures and dislocations due to muscle spasm and, most seriously, an interruption of the rhythm of the heart causing an irregular beat or stopping the heart altogether. There are also temporary effects on the nervous system such as blindness and loss of consciousness.

Treatment

1   Do not approach the casualty if he is still connected to the electric current. Make sure that the current is switched off before you touch him.

2   If the casualty is unconscious check immediately to see if he is breathing and has a pulse. If he is not breathing and/or has no pulse turn to page 12 and immediately begin the resuscitation procedures.

3   If the casualty is breathing and has a pulse but is unconscious turn to page 10 and put him into the recovery position.

4   If the casualty is conscious get him into a safe, protected place, lie him down and reassure him. Treat for shock by putting rolled-up clothing under his legs to raise them. Keep his head low: do not encourage him to sit up.

5   Look for burns on the surface and treat them by covering with a clean dressing such as a sterile dressing if the area is small, or a triangular bandage if large.

6   If he is fully conscious give two paracetamol tablets for the pain.

7   Stay with him and reassure him, checking his response every 10 minutes. If he becomes unconscious turn to page 10. If he stops breathing turn to page 12.

8   Check the casualty to see if he has any other injuries due to muscle contraction at the time of the shock. These will be fractures or dislocations. Turn to pages 46–53 for limb injury; page 42 for back injury.

If the casualty has no such injuries, is conscious and has no extensive burns there is no urgency to get him to medical attention once the electric current is switched off.

If he has other injuries or extensive burns you will need to get medical attention urgently. Turn to page 38 to assess the extent of the burns and find out how to treat the casualty until you get medical help.

➤ Always turn the power off before you approach an electric shock victim, or you may suffer an equally bad shock yourself.

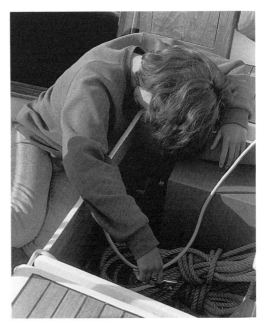

For **sunburn** turn to page 26.

For **electric burns** turn to page 37.

Burns are caused by dry heat, scalds by moist heat. In practice burns and scalds are treated in the same way.

Burns and scalds can cause several degrees of damage depending how deep the injury goes. There may be inflammation of the skin, loss of part of the thickness of the skin or loss of the whole thickness of the skin with damage to the tissues beneath. The seriousness of a burn or scald depends on the area of the skin that is affected and the depth of the injury.

Burns and scalds must be taken seriously. If nine per cent of the body area is involved the casualty will go into shock because of fluid loss, and will need urgent medical treatment as soon as possible after the accident occurs.

Treatment

1   Put on vinyl gloves from the First Aid kit.

2   Immerse the parts that have been burned or scalded in gently flowing cold water. Continue to flood with water for 10 minutes. Use drinking water or even clean seawater.

While this is being done, remove any tight clothing or jewellery from the injured area before swelling begins.

3   Help the casualty lie down and reassure him.

4   If the skin is not broken, carefully apply burn cream. If the skin *is* broken do not apply cream, but cover the injured area with a clean cloth or dressing. For a large area use one of the triangular bandages.

5   If the casualty is fully alert give him repeated warm, sweet drinks.

6   Deal with the pain. If your First Aid kit contains only paracetamol give the casualty two tablets immediately and get him to hospital as quickly as possible. If you are far offshore and it will take you many hours to get attention use the most powerful painkiller in your drug box. If you are going to give morphine or pethidine try to speak to a doctor on your radio. Turn to page 82.

7   If you are on a long passage and there is an unavoidable delay in getting the casualty to hospital lie him with his head on a small pillow and legs raised to counteract shock.

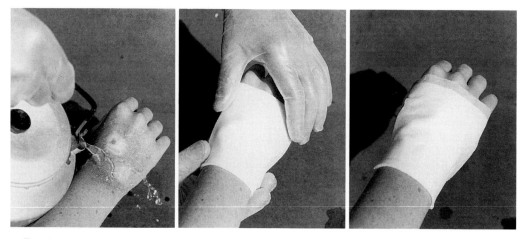

← Flood a burn with cold water for 10 minutes, and remove any tight clothing or jewellery.

Gently apply a clean dressing or cloth.

Tape the dressing in place, using ordinary adhesive tape.

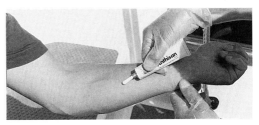

☚ Use a burn cream such as Anthisan on minor burns where the skin is not broken.

☚ Give the casualty plenty of warm, sweet drinks, and the most powerful painkillers you have on board.

ROPE BURNS

When a rope runs quickly over bare skin the heat produced by friction can cause burns while the mechanical rubbing of the rope causes tissue damage.

Treat as for burns opposite.

BURNS BY CORROSIVES

1 Immediately flood the contaminated area with water. Pour water over continuously to remove the corrosive and to cool the area. Make sure that the water drains right away and so does not contaminate anything else.

2 Remove all contaminated clothing, cutting it away if necessary. Continue to flood with water for 15 minutes. Do not burst blisters.

3 Give pain relief as suggested under *burns* above.

4 After flooding with water is completed, cover the affected area with a clean or sterile dressing.

THE SHOCK POSITION
Lie the patient flat with her head down and legs raised on pillows.

The skull surrounds the brain and protects it. The main danger of a fractured skull is that there is injury to the brain underneath. As it fractures, however, the skull absorbs a lot of energy that otherwise would have been transmitted to the brain tissue – so brain damage may be actually reduced by the skull fracturing.

It is often very difficult to diagnose a fracture of the skull without resorting to X-ray equipment, so if the casualty has had a severe blow to the head do not spend time deciding whether or not he has a fracture of the skull: simply go ahead and treat him for head injury as described on page 28.

But if you can see that a part of the skull is obviously crushed or if you can see broken bone through a wound follow these instructions.

Treatment

1 If the casualty is unconscious move him to a safe place, then put him into the recovery position as described on page 10. If there is a wound on the scalp or face place the casualty in the recovery position with the wound uppermost.

2 Once the casualty is in the recovery position and you have made sure that he is breathing, deal with the wound. First stop the bleeding as described on page 16, then treat the wound as described on page 34. Stay with the casualty to ensure that he is in a secure place and that his airway is open.

> **If you have an unconscious casualty with a head injury use the radio to get medical advice and take all steps to get the casualty ashore to hospital as quickly as possible.**

3 If the casualty is conscious take him below to a secure place where he can sit or lie comfortably. Deal with bleeding (page 16), then with any wound (page 34).

4 Turn to page 28 and follow the routine for assessing the patient's level of consciousness.

5 Get the casualty ashore as soon as possible.

➤ If the casualty is unconscious put her in the recovery position.

FRACTURES OF THE BONES OF THE FACE

There are three areas of bone in the face that can be fractured: the nasal bone, the upper jaw and the lower jaw.

Fracture of the nasal bone

The nasal bone is a very small bone, because most of the nose is made of cartilage. However, a blow to the bridge of the nose can cause a fracture; this may cause bleeding, and displaced bone or swelling may obstruct the nasal air passage. If the nasal bone is broken there will be a great deal of bruising around the eyes.

1 If the patient is unconscious deal with that first (see page 10).

2 If he is conscious sit him up, and if there is bleeding from the nose pinch the fleshy part of the nose firmly between your forefinger and thumb and maintain this pressure for 10 minutes.

3 Cover any wound (see page 34).

4 Give two paracetamol tablets every four to six hours to reduce the pain.

Fractures of the upper jaw

Fractures of the upper jaw usually involve the upper teeth or the cheek bone. These fractures are usually fairly stable, but there will be a great deal of bruising.

1 If the casualty is unconscious turn to page 10.

2 If he is conscious sit him in a secure place and treat any wounds as described on page 34.

3 If the casualty is conscious and can swallow, give two paracetamol tablets crushed in water.

Fracture of the lower jaw

1 If the casualty is unconscious turn to page 10.

2 If the casualty is conscious sit him in a secure place and support the lower jaw so that he can breathe. Keep the head well forward so that secretions drain out of the mouth.

3 If the jaw is unstable place a pad under the lower jaw, then place a bandage around the head and tie it on top of the head.

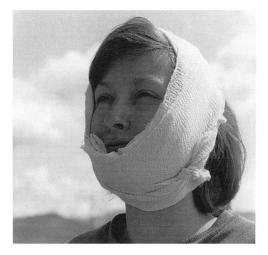

← Immobilise a broken lower jaw by placing a pad under it and holding the pad in place with a bandage tied right over the head.

The spine extends from the lower part of the skull to the bottom of the back. It consists of 33 small bones called vertebrae, linked together to form a long hollow column. The upper 24 bones are separate from each other, with flexible joints between them; the lower nine bones are fused together into a solid mass.

The hollow tube of the spine encloses the spinal cord, which conveys messages from the brain to the muscles and conveys messages back to the brain from all parts of the body. If the spinal cord is badly damaged the casualty will be paralysed and will have no feeling from that point down, so spinal injuries are very dangerous.

It follows that anyone with an injury to the back must be treated with the utmost care. Do not try to decide whether he has a fractured spine or not. Treat any casualty who has an injured back as though he *does* have a fractured spine until you are sure that he has not.

The nature of the accident will often tell you that a casualty has an injury to his back. Falling backwards onto the guard rail or onto a stone quay, being hit by the boom or falling heavily when below – all these are common causes of back injury. Falling from a height onto your feet can jar the spinal cord and even result in fractures. Diving into shallow water and landing on your head can cause severe injury to the bones at the upper end of the spine.

If you suspect a back injury ask the casualty if he can feel his arms and legs normally. Ask him to wiggle his fingers and his toes. Tell him to stay still while you lightly touch him on the trunk, arms and legs to see if he can feel your touch.

> **Do not move the casualty unless it is absolutely necessary to do so.**

Only two factors should persuade you to move a casualty with a back injury. The first is that he is in a dangerous position and must be moved because there is a risk of further injury or even death if he remains where he is.

Secondly, even if you suspect a back injury, if the casualty is unconscious and starts to vomit then he must be turned onto his side or he will inhale the vomit and drown.

If the casualty is unconscious and in a dangerous place you will have to move him and place him in the recovery position when you get him to safety.

There is a special way of moving a casualty with a back injury but this manoeuvre requires six people to achieve it. If you are at sea and there are only two of you, turn to page 10 and use the ordinary recovery position. But if you are on land and can get five helpers you will be able to use the **spinal recovery position.**

◆ The spinal recovery position: first straighten one arm . . .

And raise the other while holding the casualty's head.

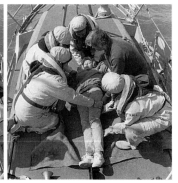

Start to roll her over, without twisting her spine . . .

1 Place the casualty's head looking straight ahead, with one person gently maintaining this by holding the head on each side. Three helpers should kneel on one side of the casualty, two on the other side.

2 Straighten the casualty's legs and bend his arm up alongside his head on the side with three helpers. Straighten his other arm along his side.

3 The three helpers should then lean over the casualty and gently roll him towards them onto his side as the other two helpers lift his back. The sixth helper gently turns the casualty's head as the others roll, supporting the head and maintaining it in the straight-ahead position with respect to the trunk. Hold it there until you can apply a neck collar.

4 Bend the casualty's lowermost arm underneath his head so that it makes his head and neck more stable.

5 Bend his uppermost leg so that his knee comes forward to make the position of the trunk more stable.

6 Make a neck collar by rolling a newspaper so it is about four inches high. Cover the rolled newspaper with a triangular bandage. Place it under the chin of the casualty, fold it around his neck and tie it in position.

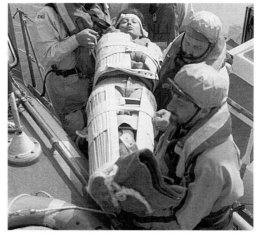

← The lifeboat is equipped with a special stretcher designed to hold the casualty's body straight.

7 Any casualty with a back injury needs to have medical attention as soon as possible, so use the radio to call the coastguard for advice and to get help.

When help is near do not start to move the casualty in readiness. The lifeboat will have trained First Aiders on board and may carry a doctor. If a helicopter comes to you leave all decisions about moving the casualty to the winchman. If you get into harbour leave the casualty on board with someone in attendance until the doctor or the ambulancemen organise the transfer.

And roll her gently into the recovery position.

Bend her upper leg to stabilise her body.

Reinforce her neck with a neck collar and radio for help.

If you suspect that someone has a chest injury get him into shelter and strip him to the waist to look for wounds that may penetrate through the chest wall to the lung. If there is a wound turn to page 30 now.

After a blow to the chest, a fall onto the chest or a crush injury the casualty may find it painful to breathe, and coughing may be excruciatingly painful. This suggests fractured ribs, especially if the pain persists after an hour or two.

Treatment

1   Put the arm on the injured side into a full arm sling (page 46).

2   Allow the casualty to find the sitting or semi-lying position that is most comfortable and which allows easy breathing. Make sure that the uninjured side is uppermost and therefore free to expand on breathing to compensate for the injured side.

3   Give two paracetamol tablets every four hours.

4   If the casualty becomes unconscious place him in the recovery position (page 10) making sure that the uninjured side is uppermost.

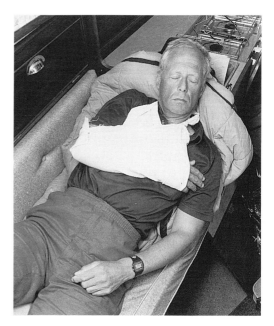

← Reduce the pain of broken ribs by putting the arm into a sling, and allow the casualty to rest in the position that gives him least discomfort.

5   If the casualty has no chest wound, is breathing fairly comfortably at rest and his lips are the normal pink colour there is no urgency to get him to hospital, but the sooner he can be offered medical care, the better.

FRACTURES OF THE PELVIS

The pelvic bones surround the lower part of the abdomen, and if the pelvis is broken, either by direct force or by falling heavily on to both feet, the internal organs of the lower abdomen may be injured as well.

The legs articulate with the pelvis at the hips, so a casualty with an injury to the pelvis may have pain on moving his legs and may be unable to stand.

Treatment

1 Lie the casualty down on his back and, if necessary, make him comfortable by placing pillows beneath his knees.

2 Give two paracetamol tablets for the pain.

3 If you have to move the casualty, either on board or, when the time comes, from the vessel to the shore or rescue craft, it is best to support the pelvis. To do this place small, soft pads between the knees and ankles, then tie the legs of the casualty together with three bandages: one bandage around the hips, one around the thighs and the third at the ankles. Make sure that the casualty rests in a secure place.

4 If he passes water, note if it is bloodstained since this may be a sign of internal injury.

5 Fracture of the pelvis is a serious injury. Seek advice by R/T and make arrangements to get the casualty ashore to medical attention as soon as possible.

To support the pelvis, pad the casualty's knees and ankles and use three bandages to strap her hips and legs as shown.

The upper limb effectively starts at the collar bone and ends at the finger tips. Most of the bones are long and slender, so fractures are common.

Do not try to decide whether a bone is broken or if there is just muscle or joint injury: that sort of diagnosis is almost impossible without the help of X-ray equipment. If the casualty has pain in the limb which does not quickly subside, or if he cannot use the limb properly, then treat the injury as a fracture until the casualty is examined by a doctor or until the limb is obviously better.

Fractures are extremely painful conditions and although fractures of the bones of the arm and the hand are not life-threatening the casualty will have considerable pain until the fracture is completely immobilised by plastering. Arrange to get the casualty to hospital as soon as possible for his own comfort.

One technique in particular is useful with almost all fractures of the upper arm: the full arm sling. The only arm injury which will prevent its use is an injury to the elbow which stops it bending.

Full arm sling
1 Take the injured arm and gently bend the elbow so that the finger tips point towards the opposite shoulder.

2 Slide a triangular bandage between the injured arm and the chest, take the bottom corner up and tie the sling on the side of the neck that the injury is on.

3 Take the third corner of the bandage, bring it forward round the elbow and pin it in position.

For many years wooden splints were used to immobilise fractures of limbs. However, they often cause discomfort and further injury, so they should be used only by a doctor or a very experienced First Aider. Inflatable splints can also cause pain and may be dangerous: they can be inflated to such an extent that they stop the circulation in the limb and cause gangrene, so do not use them on a casualty unless you have been trained in their use.

▲ The full arm sling: slip the bandage under the arm.

Take the bottom corner up and tie it to the other at the neck.

Bring the third corner around the elbow and pin it.

FRACTURE OF THE COLLAR BONE

The collar bone is commonly fractured by indirect force when the casualty falls onto the point of the shoulder. It can also be caused by a direct blow. A casualty with a broken collar bone will hold his injured arm to support it. He will complain of severe pain in the shoulder and upper arm.

1 Before you deal with the fracture always check to see if there is bleeding or a wound. Stop the bleeding (page 16) and dress any wound (page 34), then carry out the treatment for the fracture.

2 Put the injured arm into a full arm sling (page 46) with the fingers pointing towards the uninjured shoulder. Make sure that the sling is tied firmly so that the elbow is well supported. This will take the weight of the arm off the injured part and will give good pain relief.

3 Place a long bandage around the sling to hold it against the trunk for extra support.

4 Give two paracetamol tablets for pain, and repeat every four hours if necessary.

FRACTURE OF THE UPPER ARM

The single bone of the upper arm between the shoulder and elbow joints is called the humerus.

1 Before you deal with the fracture always check to see if there is bleeding or a wound. Stop the bleeding (page 16) and dress any wound (page 34), then carry out the treatment for the fracture.

2 Place the injured arm in a full arm sling (page 46).

3 Give two paracetamol tablets for the relief of pain, and repeat every four hours if necessary.

▲ A casualty with a fractured collarbone will try to relieve the weight of her arm like this.

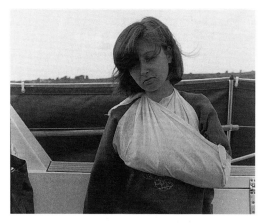

▲ Apply a full arm sling to take the weight off the collarbone . . .

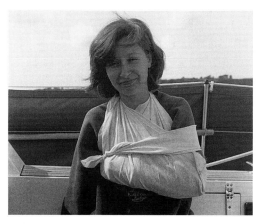

▲ And tie an extra bandage around the sling to stop it moving.

FRACTURE OF THE FOREARM OR WRIST

There are two bones in the forearm called the radius and the ulna. They lie together between the elbow and the wrist. Fractures of the wrist are usually fractures of the radius and/or ulna.

1 Before you deal with the fracture always check to see if there is bleeding or a wound. Stop the bleeding (page 16) and dress any wound (page 34), then carry out the treatment for the fracture.

2 Place the injured arm in a full arm sling (page 46).

3 Give two paracetamol tablets for the relief of pain, and repeat every four hours if necessary.

FRACTURE WHERE THE ELBOW CANNOT BE BENT

1 Help the casualty to lie down and support the injured arm straight by the side of his body.

2 Place soft padding between the injured arm and the body.

3 Use three long bandages (triangular bandages can be used) to secure the injured arm to the trunk. Do not include the uninjured arm in the bandaging.

4 Make sure that the casualty is allowed to rest in a safe place.

5 Transport by stretcher when the time comes.

INJURY TO THE HAND AND FINGERS

There are many types of injury to the hand and fingers besides fractures. Try to find out precisely what the damage is by examining the injured hand carefully. If there are crush injuries, wounds with swelling or some major deformity treat as a fracture.

1 Before you deal with a fracture always check to see if there is bleeding or a wound. Stop the bleeding (page 16) and dress any wound (page 34), then carry out the treatment for the fracture. To dress an injured finger use the finger dressing applicator and tubular dressing.

2 Place the arm in a full arm sling (page 46) with the injured hand supported as high as possible towards the uninjured shoulder.

3 Give two paracetamol tablets for the pain and repeat the dose every four hours if necessary.

♦ If the casualty cannot bend her elbow, place padding between her body and the injured arm and secure the arm like this.

◆ To dress a finger, load a tubular dressing onto the applicator and slip it over the injured finger.

◆ Slip the dressing onto the finger while withdrawing the applicator.

◆ Twist the applicator to seal the end of the dressing.

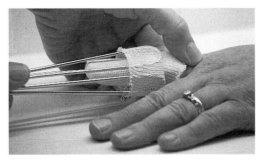

◆ Slip the remainder of the dressing onto the finger and secure it with tape.

Dressing a finger
1   Push 20 inches (50 cm) of dressing onto the applicator.

2   Place the applicator over the injured finger and transfer layers of dressing onto the injured finger by pulling and pushing the applicator backwards and forwards.

3   When you have applied four layers cut the rest of the dressing free, turn the dressing back over the finger and fix with elastoplast tape.

DISLOCATIONS

Where bones articulate with each other at a joint it is possible for one or more to be displaced so that they do not join together as they should. This injury is known as a dislocation and is caused by a force acting on the joint.

The symptoms of a dislocation are severe pain and an inability to move the joint in the normal way. These symptoms are very like the symptoms of a fracture, and indeed fractures may occur near the affected joint, caused by the accident that caused the dislocation.

Most dislocations occur at the shoulder joint, the joints of the fingers and thumb, and the lower jaw. Rarer dislocations occur at the elbow joint and the knee joint.

Never attempt to replace the bones in their normal position. This must be done by somebody with expertise, as the bones may be broken during the attempt and damage may also occur to nerves or blood vessels near the dislocated joint.

Treatment
Treat the injury as a fracture. Look up the treatment for a fracture of that part of the body and carry out the procedures described there.

It is often difficult to decide whether or not a bone is fractured, so do not try. If the casualty is in pain, or there is deformity of the limb, or he cannot move the limb properly, treat it as a fracture.

Fractures of the lower limb are common injuries. The main objects of First Aid are to take the weight off the injured limb by lying the casualty down, and then immobilise the broken limb by tying it either to the other leg or (if you know how to use them) to splints.

Wooden splints are sometimes used for fractures of the long bones of the leg, but they may cause pain and further injury. Inflatable splints are even more dangerous since they can be inflated to an extent that will stop circulation in the limb and cause gangrene.

So do not use splints unless you have had previous instruction and experience with them.

➤ To immobilise a fractured leg, tie it to the other leg using three long bandages, padding the knees and ankles.

Immobilising a fractured leg

1   Lie the casualty down. If there is bleeding or a wound, first stop the bleeding (page 16), then deal with the wound (page 34).

2   Place the limb in a reasonably comfortable position with the leg straight. This is best done by two people: one supporting the heel and foot, the other supporting the leg above and below the fracture.

3   Move the uninjured leg gently alongside the injured leg.

4   Place soft padding between the knees and the ankles of the two legs.

5   Place folded triangular bandages round the two legs to fasten them together so that the good leg acts as a splint for the broken one. Tie one bandage above the fracture and one below. Tie the third around the ankles in a figure-of-eight. Tie the bandages firmly to prevent movement.

FRACTURE OF THE HIP

This is a common fracture of elderly people and can occur after a slight stumble or minor fall. The fracture actually affects the neck of the femur, or thigh bone. The casualty will complain of pain in the hip and groin and will be quite unable to stand or walk.

1 Immobilise the patient's leg as described opposite.

2 Give two paracetamol tablets for the pain and repeat every four hours.

3 If you are on a long ocean passage and you are carrying a stronger pain killer use it as directed.

4 This is a debilitating fracture in the elderly and the casualty needs urgent hospital treatment.

➤ Someone with a fractured hip will be quite unable to stand or walk. Immobilise the leg as shown opposite.

FRACTURE OF THE THIGH

The large bone of the thigh cannot be broken without considerable damage to the surrounding tissues, involving a great deal of blood loss. The blood loss may be into the tissues of the thigh and not appear as external bleeding. The thigh will be swollen, the foot usually falls outwards and the casualty cannot move his leg.

1 Immobilise the leg as described opposite.

2 Give two paracetamol for the pain and repeat every four hours.

3 If you are on a long passage and are carrying a stronger pain killer use it as directed.

4 This is a very serious injury: the casualty may go into shock from blood loss, so make every effort to get the casualty to hospital as quickly as possible, summoning help as necessary.

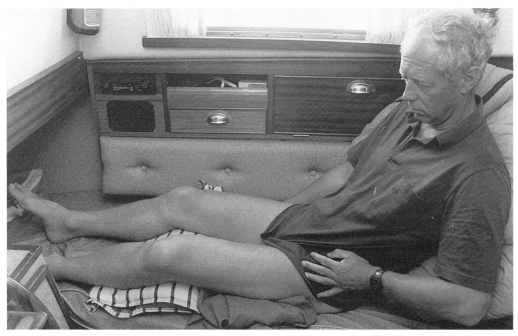

FRACTURED KNEE CAP

This is usually caused by a direct blow to the front of the knee. The fracture causes great pain and the casualty is unable to straighten his leg.

1   Lie the casualty down. If there is bleeding stop it (page 16) and then clean and cover any wound (page 34).

2   Manoeuvre the injured leg into the most comfortable position, but do not attempt to straighten it.

3   Place rolled-up clothing under the injured knee to support it. Place more clothing around the knee to keep it steady. Remember that the knee must be kept steady as the boat moves.

4   Give two paracetamol tablets every four hours. If you are carrying a stronger pain killer use that according to the instructions.

5   This is an extremely painful injury, so summon all the help you can to get the casualty to hospital as soon as possible.

FRACTURES OF THE LOWER LEG AND ANKLE

1   Immobilise the leg as described above (page 50).

2   Give two paracetamol tablets for the pain, and repeat the dose every four hours. If you are carrying a stronger pain killer use that according to the instructions.

CRUSH INJURIES TO THE FOOT

If a foot is crushed in machinery or by something falling on it there may be multiple fractures.

1   Remove the boot or shoe and sock immediately, carefully cutting them off if necessary.

2   If there is bleeding stop it (page 16), then clean and dress any wound (page 34).

3   Place padding round the injured foot and leave the casualty to rest.

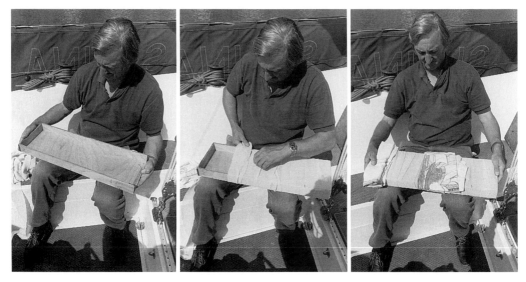

◄ You can use a drawer like this to stabilise a fractured kneecap.

Break off one end of the drawer and wrap the rest in bandages.

Then place a folded towel or spare clothing on top to pad behind the knee.

4   Give two paracetamol tablets for the pain, and repeat the dose every four hours. If you are carrying a stronger pain killer use that according to the instructions.

BROKEN TOE

This is a common injury caused by heavy objects dropping onto the toes.

1   Take off the boot or shoe and the sock.

2   If there is bleeding stop it (page 16), then clean and dress any wound (page 34).

3   Let the casualty rest with the injured foot elevated.

4   Give two paracetamol tablets for the pain, and repeat the dose every four hours.

5   If there is not a great deal of swelling after two hours it will help to put a shoe on the foot. The casualty will be able to move about with some difficulty but should elevate the foot when resting.

Secure the support under the leg with two more bandages. Note the pad under the knee.

Pain in the chest should always be regarded as serious because pain from the heart is felt in the chest. When someone complains of chest pain it is no use trying to make a diagnosis, since trying to distinguish between indigestion and a heart attack often takes a team of doctors two days. If somebody has a pain in the chest which seems to them to be out of the ordinary treat him as though he has had a heart attack.

1 Take the casualty to a safe place and let him choose the position which he feels is most comfortable. Do not try to make him lie down flat if he feels better sitting up. Anyone with severe chest pain will feel weak and may find it difficult to breathe, so make sure that there is good ventilation to prevent him feeling suffocated.

2 Reassure him, offer him sips of water and give him two paracetamol tablets. If you are on a long ocean passage and you are carrying pain killers which are stronger than paracetamol you may think about using them for chest pain. Use them as instructed by the doctor who prescribed them – but only if the chest pain is severe and does not ease when the patient has rested for 10 minutes.

3 After severe chest pain, and even if the pain becomes less severe after a while, keep the patient resting until you can get him ashore to a doctor.

4 Radio ashore for advice and call the emergency services to get the patient to medical care as quickly as possible.

5 Once the patient feels better you may give him small snacks and drinks every four hours or so but don't give large meals.

> If the patient becomes unconscious it is likely that he has had a cardiac arrest. Turn to page 12 and begin resuscitation immediately.

ANGINA

Angina is the term to describe a pain in the chest which may come on after exercise which causes the heart to work harder. The pain of angina goes away quickly once the patient rests by sitting or lying down.

If a crew member has an angina attack treat him as above for chest pain. Many sufferers carry a spray or tablets to take if they have an attack; if this is the case get the patient's medication and help him to take a dose. Make sure that the patient rests for the remainder of the passage.

➤ The best thing you can do for someone with chest pain is to provide him with rest and reassurance.

A stroke occurs when the blood supply to part of the brain is suddenly cut off by a clot in an artery or by a haemorrhage from an artery. In either case events happen quickly hence the name "stroke". The rapidity of the stroke and its effects depend on the severity of the bleeding and the part of the brain that is involved.

Symptoms
- The patient may complain of a sudden headache or giddiness.
- He may not be able to speak or his words may be jumbled so that they do not make sense.
- His face may be distorted on one side and he may even be paralysed on one or both sides.
- He may lose control of his bladder and bowels.

After a stroke the symptoms and signs may stay the same or the patient may gradually sink into unconsciousness.

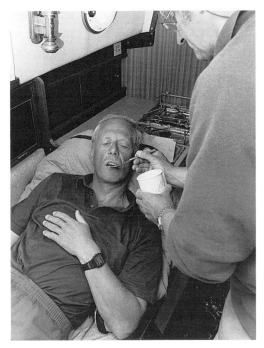

◆ If you have to feed a stroke victim give him liquid food, since he may choke on solids.

Treatment
1 Get the patient below to a safe place where he can rest. Make sure he is wedged into a berth and cannot fall: remember that he may be very giddy.

2 Lie him down with his head on a pillow and reassure him. Stay with him and regularly assess his responsiveness by talking to him and asking simple questions (see page 28). Do not give him anything by mouth if you know that you are going to get the patient to medical attention within a few hours.

3 If the patient becomes unconscious turn to page 10 and follow the routine for dealing with an unconscious casualty.

4 Once you have the patient in the recovery position make sure he is securely wedged against the movement of the boat so he cannot fall on his face and suffocate. If you have to leave him to help with the running of the boat make sure that you go below at least once every 10 minutes to see that he is safe.

5 A stroke is always a dangerous illness since you cannot tell whether the bleeding into the brain will stop or not. You should make every effort to get advice by R/T and get the patient ashore to hospital as soon as possible.

If you are many miles from help on a long passage you will need to look after the patient for the whole time. If it is going to be days before you get to help and the patient is conscious you will have to give him drinks or he will become dehydrated. You may have to feed him with spoonfuls of liquid. Do not give solid food as the patient may not be able to swallow properly and may choke.

If he is unconscious do not attempt to give anything to eat or drink.

The patient may not be able to control his bladder and bowels, in which case gently clean him up and change his clothes.

Asthma is a condition that creates difficulty in breathing because the air passages in the chest have constricted and will not allow free movement of air to and from the lungs. An attack may be triggered by nervous tension or by allergy, but very often there seems to be no obvious reason for it.

Many people suffer from asthma and most of them carry their own medication – sometimes tablets, more often inhalers – that they can use whenever they feel an attack coming on. But it is easy, in the rush of getting to sea, for an asthma sufferer to forget his inhaler. This can cause real problems because the person feels so unprotected without his medication that the stress precipitates an attack.

If you know that one of the crew has asthma, remind him to take his inhaler with him. If you get to sea and find that the inhaler has been left behind go back for it, unless the crew member can be sure that any possible attack will be mild.

Note If you are setting out on an ocean passage any crew member who has asthma attacks must make sure that he carries sufficient medication for the longest time that the passage may take.

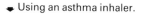
◄ Using an asthma inhaler.

◄ The feel of fresh air will speed the recovery of anyone suffering an asthma attack.

Treatment

1 Sit the patient down and allow him to find the most comfortable position for himself. Usually he will lean forward with his arms braced to help breathing.

2 Reassure the patient constantly. Make sure that there is a pronounced draught so that the patient knows that there is plenty of air to breathe.

3 Get any medication that the patient has on board and allow him to take a dose. Stay with him and calmly reassure him. Many attacks will stop after this treatment and the patient will be able to breathe easily again. After a few minutes' rest he will be able to carry on normally.

5 Some attacks are not so easily dealt with, and occasionally prove fatal, so if the attack persists for more than hour call for help on the radio and prepare to get the patient to medical attention.

An allergy develops when a person becomes sensitised to a substance and reacts in an abnormal manner when he comes into contact with it. Perhaps the best known allergy is hay fever. Many people can come into contact with grass pollen without reacting to it at all, but others develop streaming eyes and nose whenever there is pollen in the air because their mucous membranes react abnormally to its presence.

Moderate allergic reactions usually affect the skin and the mucous membranes; they result only in uncomfortable rashes and running eyes and nose. More severe allergic reactions involve the muscles of the air passages, giving rise to asthma or – more seriously – anaphylactic shock. In anaphylactic shock the casualty will develop a massive reaction very quickly after an insect sting or the injection of a drug.

MODERATE ALLERGY

Anthisan cream will soothe a skin rash. A simple eye wash can help in cases of hay fever. Paracetamol will reduce the irritation (two tablets every four hours).

ANAPHYLACTIC SHOCK

Shortly after an insect sting or after taking a drug to which the casualty is sensitised he will feel sick and vomit. He will complain that his chest feels tight and that it is hard to breathe. There may be swelling around his eyes and he may sneeze. He will become faint and giddy.

Treatment

1 Lie the casualty down and raise his legs by putting them on a pile of clothes. Do not put a pillow under the casualty's head.

2 Loosen tight clothing.

3 Reassure the casualty, stay with him and cover him with a blanket to prevent cooling.

4 If his breathing becomes difficult or the casualty becomes unconscious place him in the recovery position (page 10).

5 If his breathing stops carry out resuscitation (page 12).

6 Make every effort to get the casualty ashore to medical attention as quickly as possible.

The shock position: head down and legs raised.

When internal bleeding occurs the source of the bleeding is in one of the internal organs of the body, so it cannot be reached by a First Aider. Because of this it cannot be stopped by direct pressure. However, blood from internal bleeding may reach the surface of the body, giving some clues to its origin. If the casualty vomits blood or passes bloodstained or black "tarry" motions there is bleeding into the stomach or the bowel. If the casualty coughs up blood the bleeding is in the lungs. If he passes blood in the urine there is internal bleeding from the kidneys, bladder or urethra. Abnormal bleeding from the vagina may be due to internal bleeding from the womb. But beware: some internal bleeding, into the abdominal cavity or into the muscles surrounding a broken bone, does not come to the surface and cannot be seen.

If sufficient blood is lost the general symptoms and signs will be the same, whether the bleeding is internal or external. The casualty will feel weak, giddy and faint and will become anxious and restless. He will look pale with a cold sweat. His pulse will become increasingly rapid as he loses more and more blood.

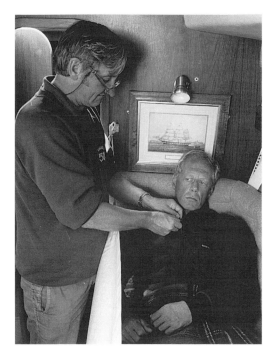

← If you suspect internal bleeding, help the patient below, get him to lie down and loosen his clothing.

← Raise his legs a little and encourage him to lie still. Reassure him.

Treatment

1   Lie the casualty down in the warmest, most comfortable place. Reassure the casualty and keep him lying still even when he is restless. Raise his legs by placing a mass of rolled-up clothing under them.

2   If the casualty complains of cold, cover him with a sleeping bag or blanket.

3   If you are far offshore and it is going to be several hours before the casualty receives medical attention give him sips of warm drinks if he is thirsty. If you are within four hours of getting him to hospital give nothing by mouth.

4   If the casualty becomes unconscious put him in the recovery position (page 10).

5   Internal bleeding is always dangerous since it is impossible to predict whether it will stop, continue or become more severe, with possible danger to life. So you must make every effort to get the casualty to medical attention as soon as possible.

☛ Cover him with a sleeping bag or blanket if he is cold. If you are a long way offshore, give sips of warm drinks.

☛ If he becomes unconscious put him in the recovery position (page 10).

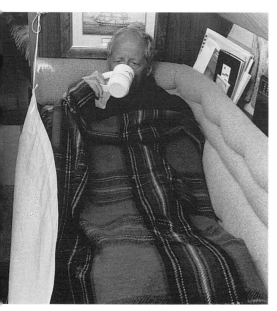

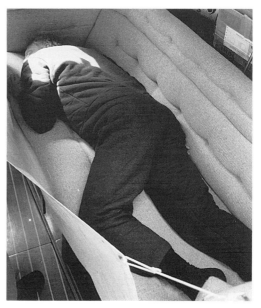

A patient with diabetes has lost control of the amount of sugar in his bloodstream. If his blood sugar level rises as a result he will become hot, dry and drowsy, and eventually he will become unconscious and die.

For many people with diabetes the only way to keep the blood sugar within normal limits is to take insulin regularly. But sometimes the insulin taken more than compensates for the excess sugar in the blood and the blood sugar level drops too low.

The first type of imbalance, where the blood sugar level is too high, is called a diabetic crisis. The second, where the blood sugar is too low, is known as an insulin crisis.

Diabetic crisis

If the patient does not take enough insulin his blood sugar will gradually rise over three or four days. He will pass great quantities of urine as his body tries to eliminate the sugar, he will be thirsty and his skin will be dry and hot. Eventually he will not be able to excrete the sugar fast enough, his blood sugar level will rise and gradually he will become sleepy. Eventually he will lapse into coma.

This often occurs if a diabetic has an infection such as tonsillitis or a boil. The infection upsets the sugar balance and the patient needs more insulin; if he doesn't get enough insulin a diabetic crisis will develop.

Insulin crisis

If a diabetic takes his normal dose of insulin but either does not eat or uses up more energy than usual he may start to suffer from a low blood sugar level. He will feel faint and may become aggressive. He will be pale and his skin will feel clammy and cold. He will be restless and will become unconscious in a matter of an hour or two.

At sea this type of crisis may be precipitated by the patient not eating because of nausea and actual seasickness, or by the unaccustomed physical activity which uses up blood sugar.

Prevention

If you take insulin you should take certain precautions if you are going to sea. You should be aware that you may suffer from seasickness and be unable to eat, so it might be wise to use seasickness prevention measures as described on page 24. You should also be aware that you use a lot more energy than usual while sailing, so you should carry boiled sweets or sweet drinks to take at the first sign of faintness. You must be aware that ordinary infections often crop up when you are far offshore so it is a good idea to have a chat with your doctor and perhaps carry suitable antibiotics when you go to sea so that, if necessary, you can start the course before you get ashore.

← Taken in good time, sweet foods such as chocolate may prevent the onset of an insulin crisis caused by abnormal physical activity.

Obviously it is essential to take adequate supplies of insulin – bearing in mind that you may be away longer than planned – and remember to take a blood or urine testing kit so that a clear idea of how much the blood sugar is rising can be obtained.

Treatment: insulin crisis

1 If a person with diabetes starts to behave strangely, feels faint or becomes aggressive, incoherent or unsteady, get him to a safe position and immediately give him a pint of a watery non-alcoholic drink sweetened with three tablespoonsful of sugar while he is still conscious.

2 Stay with the patient and if there is an improvement after the sweet drink give more of the same.

3 If the patient becomes cold and clammy and becomes unconscious before you can give him a sugary drink, or if you are able to test a sample of his urine or blood and the sugar is below normal, you must get him to medical care as soon as possible.

Treatment: diabetic crisis

1 If a person with diabetes becomes lethargic, feels hot and dry to the touch and does not respond to the sugary drink get him to test his urine or blood for sugar immediately.

2 If the sample contains more sugar than normal do not give him anything sweet but give plenty of unsweetened drinks and get the patient to medical care as quickly as possible.

If a person who has diabetes becomes unconscious do not try to give him anything by mouth. Treat him as an unconscious casualty as described on page 10. Use the radio to get advice and summon help. This is a serious medical emergency.

Infections are caused by viruses or bacteria invading the body. They may remain localised, as in the case of skin infections (see page 73), or they may spread into the bloodstream and cause systemic infection. Many infections cause both local and systemic effects. Influenza, for example, causes symptoms in the nose and throat as well as a generalised illness.

Symptoms of generalised infection

The patient will be flushed and hot at first, but later he will become pale, feel cold and may suffer bouts of uncontrollable shivering. He will sweat, even when resting, and he will feel parched and thirsty. Often there will be nausea or vomiting. The patient feels tired, weak and giddy, and any small task is a great effort. He will often have a headache and may have joint pains.

As the patient sweats profusely and often cannot drink copious quantities because of nausea, his urine output falls and the urine is scanty and very dark.

If you have a thermometer you may take his temperature by placing the thermometer under his tongue and asking him to close his lips around it without biting it. Normal body temperature is 98.4°F or 37°F.

Obviously somebody who has a systemic infection with the symptoms I have listed presents a frightening picture to the rest of the crew, especially if you are offshore and not likely to get to medical attention for 24 hours or more. But there is no need to be unduly worried, since with a little care the patient can be kept comfortable and safe. There is no reason to take risks to get to shore.

Treatment

1   Rest the patient in a secure berth. If he is nauseated make sure he has a bucket to hand.

2   Make sure he is dressed as normal for the conditions. Although the patient may be hot, or may go through bouts of feeling cold and shivering, he should wear the sort of clothes that a healthy person would wear. At night zip him into a sleeping bag in the normal way, but if it is hot during the day let him lie on top of the bag if he wants to. Keep that part of the boat well ventilated, but try to maintain a normal temperature.

3   Make sure that he has as much watery fluid as he can drink.

4   Give him paracetamol to bring down his temperature, since this will make him feel much better. Give two paracetamol tablets every four hours as long as his temperature is 100°F or 38°C or above. If you do not have a thermometer, continue as long as he feels hot to the touch or complains of headache.

Antibiotics

If you are planning an ocean crossing or sailing in a part of the world where it is difficult to find medical aid you will need to take antibiotics to treat severe infections. All antibiotics are available only on prescription in Britain so you will have to discuss this with your doctor.

There are many types of antibiotic. You should take one that is effective against a wide variety of infections and which is acceptable to most people. At the present time I would advise one of the 4-quinolone ring antibiotics such as ciprofloxacin. A course of these tablets is expensive but effective, and most people can take it without serious side-effects.

If you take an antibiotic with you make sure that the bottle or packet is labelled with the name and strength.

When to give antibiotics

1   Only if you are 48 hours away from medical aid – otherwise wait to see the doctor.

2   Only if the patient has been ill for more than 24 hours and has a generalised severe infection with the signs and symptoms described on these pages.

Young children react to infection more vigorously than adults. A child's temperature rises more quickly and to a higher level. He will not complain of headache as often as an adult, but he is more likely to be sick.

The infection that causes the fever in children may be bacterial like tonsillitis, or viral like measles and chickenpox. But whatever the cause the First Aid treatment is the same.

Treatment

1 Take off all the child's clothes and sponge him all over with tepid water for five minutes. Tepid water is not ice cold but it still feels cold to the touch, so the child may resist this treatment, but don't be discouraged. If his temperature is very high he may steam as the water is sponged on. This method is the quickest way to bring down the child's temperature.

2 Dress him in his ordinary nightclothes and put him to bed in a well ventilated place.

3 Give a dose of paracetamol elixir (Calpol) which contains 120 mg of paracetamol in every 5 ml:
- *Children under one year:*
  give one teaspoonful (5 ml).
- *Children between one and five years:*
  give two teaspoonsful (10 ml).
- *Children over five years:*
  give three teaspoonsful (15 ml).

4 Let the child sleep.

5 If his temperature rises to above 101°F or 38°C, or if you have no thermometer but can feel him getting hotter, repeat the tepid sponging.

6 Repeat the paracetamol only after four hours have elapsed since the last dose.

7 Make every effort to get a child with a high temperature ashore.

Epilepsy is a condition involving a temporary change in the electrical activity of the brain. This may cause only momentary loss of concentration, or it may cause a fit in which the patient loses consciousness and suffers the multiple muscle spasms or a convulsion.

Obviously it is extremely dangerous for someone to have any sort of fit on board a boat because even a minor fit can cause him to lose concentration and fall overboard.

Treatment

1   Make the patient secure.

2   Immediately protect his head with your hands. Hold his head but do not restrain its movement: just make sure it does not bang against any hard objects.

3   When the convulsing stops put the patient into the recovery position (page 10).

4   Treat any injuries that have occurred during the fit.

5   When the patient regains consciousness make sure that he remains in a secure, safe place. Stay with him, because he may behave irrationally for a short time.

6   If the patient is known to have epilepsy and has had fits before there is no reason to make a great fuss. The patient will know what to do afterwards and will prefer the passage to carry on as planned.

7   If the patient takes a long time to regain consciousness – more than an hour – or has more than one fit, you must get medical aid as quickly as possible.

CHILDREN

A child who has a high temperature may eventually have a fit. If so, treat as above and bring the child's temperature down by tepid sponging (see previous page).

☛ If someone is having a fit, hold her head to stop it banging into anything hard such as a cleat or winch.

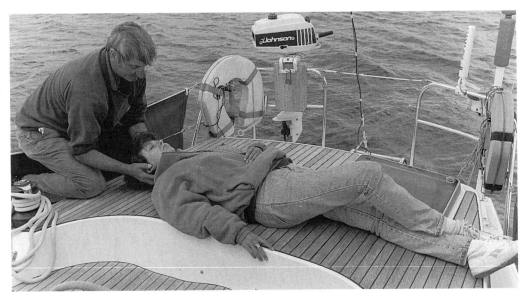

FAINTS

A person will faint if a sudden drop in blood pressure reduces the blood supply to the brain. Initially his pulse is usually slow, he feels cold and clammy and may feel sick. Then, suddenly, he will lose consciousnes.

Treatment

1 Do not attempt to hold him up, but immediately put him into the recovery position (see page 10) and wait for him to recover.

2 Make sure he is in a secure place and stay with him until you are sure that he can look after himself.

3 A patient who has fainted may twitch a little, so protect his head.

4 Faints occur for a number of reasons and the patient usually makes a full recovery after a short rest.

● When the fit has subsided put the sufferer into the recovery position until she regains consciousness.

CONSTIPATION

When going to sea for an offshore passage or an ocean crossing the change of routine can often lead to constipation. The change of diet and possible lack of fibre can also be a factor. This condition is of little importance and it does no harm to be constipated for a week or so. Drink plenty of watery fluids, eat fresh or tinned fruit and completely forget about it.

PILES

Piles (haemorrhoids) are small varicose veins at the anus. They can become swollen, and will then itch and be sore. They are of no importance, but they can be kept in check by making sure that the patient does not become constipated (see above).

Thrombosed piles
These occur when one or more of the distended veins develops a blood clot. The result is a hard lump the size of a grape at the entrance to the anus. This condition is intensely painful with a great deal of muscle spasm. The pain is often worse when the patient moves around and also after the bowels are opened.

To treat this, give two paracetamol tablets every four hours for the pain. Bathing with hot water gives the most immediate relief; if there is no bath to hand, use a flannel soaked in water as hot as the patient can stand it.

Bleeding from piles
Piles often bleed. The blood is usually bright red and appears after defaecation or wiping. Usually this condition needs no First Aid treatment, although the patient should consult his own doctor after returning home. If there is persistant bleeding from piles use cold compresses until the bleeding stops. After a bleed make sure that the patient does not become constipated by giving him plenty of fluids to drink and fresh fruit to eat.

RETENTION OF URINE

Older men sometimes find that they cannot pass water owing to an obstruction at the exit from the bladder. The patient develops discomfort, then pain as his bladder fills and becomes distended.

Treatment
1   Give two paracetamol tablets for the pain.

2   Sit the patient in a bath of warm water. If this is not possible the patient should bathe the lower part of his abdomen and his penis with warm water.

3   Allow the patient to sit undisturbed on the lavatory: eventually he may relax sufficiently to be able to urinate.

4   Give him nothing to eat or drink until he manages to urinate. Once he has passed a large amount of urine give him sips of liquid. He should pass water frequently, and not allow his bladder to become full.

5   If the patient simply cannot pass water he must be put ashore as quickly as possible. Radio for assistance. Give him two paracetamol every four hours.

RUPTURE (HERNIA)

A rupture is a protrusion of the contents of the abdomen through the muscles of the trunk wall. Ruptures appear in the groin and around the navel; they can also appear in the scars of operations.

A rupture may be discovered simply as a painless swelling or it may be painful.

Treatment

1   Make the patient lie down on his back and relax with his legs drawn up.

2   If the rupture does not go back on its own, do not try to push it back: you might make the injury worse.

3   If the patient is in pain give two paracetamol tablets every four hours.

Ruptures that are painless and go back on their own when the patient lies down are not likely to cause trouble so there is no urgency to get medical aid. But make sure he avoids heavy work such as lifting. He should seek medical attention once ashore.

▲ A hernia patient should lie down on his back with his legs raised on a heap of clothing.

Ruptures that do not go back are more dangerous. They are said to be strangulated, which means that there is bowel stuck in the swelling. This bowel may become obstructed or the bowel may be damaged by pressure. If the rupture will not go back you must get the patient ashore to medical attention as soon as possible.

Food poisoning is an irritation of the bowel caused by a living micro-organism, or by the toxic products of such an organism. The condition may begin with nausea and vomiting, then progress to diarrhoea. The stomach and bowel are over-active and the churning of the bowel makes the patient feel very weak. Typically there is a drop in blood pressure, the patient becomes pale and comes out in a cold sweat.

Generally speaking the more sudden and violent the onset of food poisoning, the quicker it will be over. Many remedies involve using drugs to calm the bowel, but this approach is usually counter-productive because the calmed bowel does not expel the cause of the trouble. As soon as the drug treatment is stopped the condition returns, so these gastrointestinal sedatives only postpone the diarrhoea and may even make it worse.

Treatment

The First Aid treatment of any form of diarrhoea should aim to make the patient as comfortable as possible and to replace the fluid that is lost.

1   Put the patient below with a bucket to hand if he is feeling sick or actually vomiting.

2   Give lots of watery drinks, encouraging many sips rather than large gulps. Even if the patient is vomiting some of the liquid will be absorbed.

3   If he is not nauseated there is no good reason to withhold food. It is not necessary to add the misery of hunger to the discomfort of diarrhoea.

4   Comfort the patient with the general rule that the more violent the diarrhoea the sooner it will be over.

ANTIBIOTICS FOR DIARRHOEA

If you are undertaking an ocean crossing and simply cannot get medical attention it is best to take courses of an antibiotic with you in case of severe debilitating gastro-enteritis. Take one of the 4-quinolone ring antibiotics such as ciprofloxacin. This drug is available by prescription only in the UK.

Children

Diarrhoea and vomiting are more serious in babies and children that they are in adults. Children have less body mass, so they become dehydrated more quickly than adults.

If a child between the ages of two and ten years goes more than 48 hours without adequate fluid intake he will become dehydrated, especially if he has watery diarrhoea as well. If the child is not vomiting and can keep down fluids then there is no fear of dehydration provided he is given lots of watery drinks. If the child is not able to keep fluids down it is essential to get him to medical treatment within 48 hours.

In babies under two years it is even more important to maintain water intake. If a baby is vomiting and cannot keep fluids down he must have medical assessment and treatment after 24 hours.

⯈ Give plenty of watery drinks to counteract the loss of body fluids that could lead to dehydration.

There are many causes of abdominal pain, and a First Aider cannot be expected to make a diagnosis.

- If the pain is accompanied by diarrhoea treat as above.

- If there is no diarrhoea and the pain is severe do not give anything by mouth.

Appendicitis always comes to mind when there is severe abdominal pain, but appendicitis is in fact quite rare. If it does occur there will usually be time to get the patient ashore for treatment before it becomes serious. Treat as below.

1 Get the patient below and make him comfortable. Usually the most comfortable position is with the patient sitting up with a pillow or bundle of clothing under his knees to support them.

2 If the patient becomes pale and clammy and feels faint remove the supports and lay him in the shock position. Do this by laying the patient flat on his back with no pillow, then raising his legs by putting rolled-up clothing under the feet and ankles.

▲ If the patient feels faint and becomes pale and clammy get her to lie down in the shock position, with her head down and legs raised.

3 If the patient is female she will know if the pain is due to her period or if it is possible that the pain is due to some complication of pregnancy. If this is the case turn to page 79.

How serious is abdominal pain? It can be caused by food poisoning or indigestion which are not usually serious. The sign of a more serious cause is persistent pain which settles in one part of the abdomen, and which becomes worse if the patient moves – that is, sits up or walks about. If the pain is severe and lasts for more than three hours it must be considered serious, and you should make every effort to get the patient to hospital as soon as possible.

POISONS SWALLOWED

The commonest way for poisons to be taken into the body is through the mouth and into the stomach. From the stomach the poison gets into the bloodstream and can then exert its effects on different organs.

Treatments

1 If the casualty is unconscious place him in the recovery position and follow the instructions for dealing with an unconscious casualty (see page 10).

2 If the casualty is conscious, first decide if the poison is corrosive or non-corrosive. You may know what the casualty has swallowed, but if you don't, have a look at the casualty's lips and mouth to see if they have been burned.

3 If you think that the casualty has swallowed a corrosive poison and he is fully alert give him sips of water or milk to soothe the burning. Place him in the recovery position and stay with him.

4 Even if you think that the poison is non-corrosive but you can get the casualty to medical attention quickly treat him as above by placing him in the recovery position and staying with him.

5 If you are several hours from any medical help and the casualty has swallowed a non-corrosive poison within the last hour, and is fully alert, you should make him sick. The best way to do this is to put your finger or the handle of a spoon to the back of the casualty's throat. This is a barbarous procedure but if it makes the casualty vomit up a dangerous poison which would otherwise be absorbed into the bloodstream it could save his life. Do not try to make the casualty sick by giving salt water: it doesn't work and it may cause the poison to be absorbed more quickly.

6 After the casualty has vomited put him into the recovery position and stay with him.

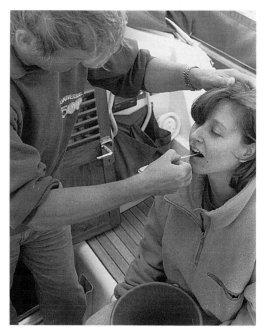

← Making someone sick may be the best way to deal with a non-corrosive poison.

POISONING THROUGH THE SKIN

Some poisons such as some pesticides can be absorbed through the skin and cause serious illness later.

Treatment

1 Lie the casualty down to rest.

2 Remove any contaminated clothing, being careful not to contaminate yourself.

3 Wash the contaminated area of skin with plenty of water – sea water will do. Make sure the water drains away and does not contaminate anything else.

4 If the casualty is unconscious place him in the recovery position (page 10).

5 If the casualty is not breathing immediately turn to page 12 and start resuscitation procedures.

POISONING BY INHALATION

Poisonous gases are absorbed from the lungs after being breathed in. Once they get into the bloodstream they can affect other organs, especially the brain.

Treatment

1 Open all doors and windows, hatches and portholes, and get the casualty away from the poisonous gas into a healthy atmosphere.

2 If the casualty is conscious and breathing let him recover in the fresh air.

3 If the casualty is unconscious but breathing place him in the recovery position (page 10) in the fresh air.

4 If the casualty is not breathing turn to page 12 immediately and carry out resuscitation procedures.

➡ If someone is suffering gas poisoning drag her into clear air before attempting any resuscitation procedures.

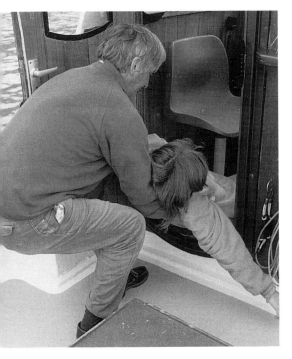

ALCOHOLIC POISONING

Alcohol is a drug that affects the brain. Small amounts cause minor changes in mood, but moderate or large quantities may cause major changes and impairment of physical performance. Very large amounts of alcohol cause unconsciousness and death.

Alcohol is particularly dangerous at sea because it affects the sense of balance and frequently causes people to fall overboard or overturn a dinghy. Once a drunken person has fallen into the water he is soon in difficulty, often vomiting with the exertion and the shock. He is much more likely to drown than a sober person.

Treatment

1 If a crew member is drunk, leave him ashore rather than letting him go out to the boat in a dinghy. If he is drunk on board make him stay below in a safe place to sleep it off, and do not allow him on deck.

2 If a drunken crew member is below in his berth, check him regularly to see that he is in the recovery position (page 10). Make sure his airway is clear and that he is breathing.

3 If somebody who has taken drink is unrousable you need medical help, because this lowered level of consciousness shows that the vital centres of the brain are being affected by the alcohol and the patient could die.

WARNING
Some poisons act hours or days after they are absorbed. Any casualty who has taken in poison by any route must be taken to medical care for assessment as soon as possible.

In Europe insect bites and stings usually give rise to a local reaction around the site with redness, pain and itching.

Some people become sensitised to certain stings and may suffer a generalised reaction and collapse.

Treatment: normal reaction

1 Look at the site to see if the sting has been left in the skin of the casualty. If it has, take a knife and gently scrape the sting out of the skin with the blade. Do not get hold of the sting to pull it out, as this may inject more venom into the casualty.

2 If there is no sting in the skin, or if you have removed it, cover the site with antihistamine cream and give two paracetamol tablets for the pain. It may take two or three days for the pain and irritation to disappear.

Collapse after a bite or sting

Some people are very sensitive to insect venom and will collapse after what, to most people, would be a harmless sting. This form of collapse, called anaphylactic shock, is a serious condition that requires immediate treatment. The casualty will complain of being unable to breathe, and will become faint, pale and clammy. Often he will lose consciousness.

1 If the casualty becomes unconscious, turn to page 12 immediately and carry out the resuscitation procedures.

2 Allow the patient to rest. Once the casualty recovers from anaphylactic shock he will usually return to normal health over the next 24 hours.

3 Get the patient ashore to hospital as quickly as possible.

FISH BITES AND STINGS

There are several fish and other marine animals that can sting if they are handled or trodden on in shallow water or on a beach.

Such stings can cause a very severe local reaction with excruciating pain, or they can have a generalised effect.

Treatment

1 If the casualty is fully conscious and breathing normally treat the sting with antihistamine cream.

2 Give two paracetamol tablets for the pain.

3 If the casualty complains of difficulty with breathing or becomes unconscious start resuscitation right away. Turn to page 12.

4 If the casualty is fully conscious you may relieve the pain by placing the affected hand or foot into hot water. The water needs to be as hot as the casualty can stand. This often reduces the pain quickly. In any event with the common jellyfish stings and weaver fish stings the pain will fade in about one hour.

SNAKE BITES

There are poisonous snakes in most parts of the world, but the most dangerous are found in the tropics. The First Aid treatment is the same for all snake bites.

Treatment

1 Lie the casualty down and reassure him.

2 Immobilise the limb or part of the trunk that was bitten.

3 Wash the bite in plenty of water. Make the water soapy if there is soap to hand, but otherwise use water alone. Wash the affected area gently, and do not rub vigorously.

4 Even if the casualty seems well, make arrangements to get him to hospital as soon as possible.

5 If you can see the snake try to remember its markings so that you can describe it at hospital. If you kill the snake take it with you for identification.

SKIN INFECTIONS

Infections of the skin are common. Small wounds can become infected or infections can form in the skin and become boils and styes.

Infected wounds should be treated by thorough cleaning, then covering with a sterile, or if that is not available, a clean dressing. See page 34 for the treatment of wounds.

STYES

Styes are infections in small glands on the eyelids. They must not be cut or lanced as this can lead to permanent scarring. They are not actually eye infections, so although they may be very painful they will not affect the patient's sight in the long term. They can cause temporary problems with vision because the swelling closes the eye, but once the swelling goes down and the eye opens the patient's sight will be normal.

Treatment

1 Give two paracetamol for the pain and repeat the dose every four hours if necessary.

2 Place hot compresses on the eyelid: put hot water onto a clean cloth and hold it over the infection until it cools, then repeat. The compress should be as hot as the patient can stand. This will soothe the pain and increase the blood supply to the eyelid, thus increasing the speed with which the infection is cleared.

3 Cover the infected eye with a clean pad.

BOILS

Boils, also known as carbuncles and abscesses, can occur anywhere on the skin. They are infections characterised by painful swelling.

Do not lance (cut) a boil because although you may release the pus and relieve the pain you may puncture something important such as a blood vessel. You may also make a nasty scar.

Treatment

1 Treat with hot compresses (see above under styes), then cover with elastoplast.

2 Wait for the boil to burst, then wash the area thoroughly with hot water and dress with clean dressing.

3 Wash and dress the area every day.

➤ Do not attempt to lance a boil: wait for it to burst, then wash and dress it.

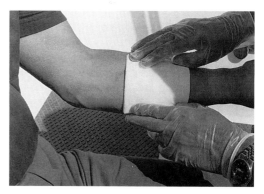

EYE DISEASES

The only common disease of the eye that you are likely to have to deal with on an offshore or ocean passage is conjunctivitis. This is an infection of the mucous membrane around the eye; the white of the eye becomes red and inflamed, there may be pus running from the eye and it is sore or itchy.

Treatment

1   Wash the eye with clean water. Drop four Predsol N eyedrops into the eye and repeat every four hours.

2   Ask the patient to close the eye, then place a soft eye pad over the whole eye. Fasten the pad with adhesive tape (e.g. Sellotape or Scotch tape).

3   If you are at sea for more than a day remove the pad several times each day, clean the eye and re-cover it with a clean pad.

4   Although this is not a dangerous condition it is uncomfortable and worrying, so the patient should get to medical treatment as soon as possible.

FOREIGN BODY IN THE EYE

If a small particle rests on the white of the eye, the coloured iris or the pupil and sticks there it will cause severe irritation and pain. A common type of foreign body in the eye is a metal fragment which flies into the eye when metal is being wire-brushed. The white of the eye will become red and the conunctiva (the rim of the eye) may swell. The casualty finds it difficult to keep the eye open and it is painful.

Treatment

1   Hold the eye open and swill the eye with clean water to float the particle out.

2   If this does not move the particle and you can clearly see it, you can try to dislodge it with the corner of a soft cloth. Be gentle, for any graze on the coloured part of the eye or the pupil can lead to permanent scarring. If you do not succeed in moving the particle with gentle movements of the cloth do not persist.

3   If you remove the particle and the casualty can open the eye easily, let the eye remain open. Drop four Predsol N eyedrops into the eye and repeat every four hours.

4   If you cannot remove the particle, or if the eye is still sore after the body has been removed, ask the casualty to close the eye. Cover it with a pad and tape the pad in place with Sellotape (Scotch tape).

5   Give two paracetamol for pain if necessary.

6   Get the casualty to medical attention as soon as possible, since a foreign body left in the eye for several days may cause scarring and loss of vision.

CORROSIVE CHEMICALS IN THE EYE

This will usually be a liquid which is spilled or squirts into the eye, causing intense pain.

Treatment

1   Hold the eye open and pour copious amounts of clean water over it to dilute and wash away the chemical. Continue until you are sure that the chemical has been washed away. Drop four Predsol N eyedrops into the eye and repeat every four hours.

2   Ask the casualty to close the eye, cover it with a pad and fix the pad with Sellotape (Scotch tape).

3   Give two paracetamol for the pain.

4   If the pain is intense close and cover the good eye in the same way.

5   You must get the casualty to medical treatment as soon as possible if the sight of the eye is to be saved.

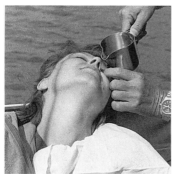

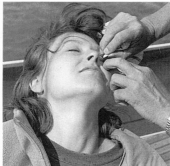

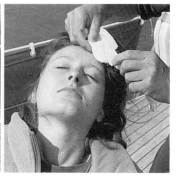

← Try to wash a foreign body out of the eye with clean water.

If this fails, try to dislodge it with a soft cloth.

If the eye remains sore, close it and cover it with a pad.

MECHANICAL INJURY TO THE EYE

Damage to the eye by a hard blow or a penetrating injury is always serious. Not only is the sight of the injured eye at risk but a so-called sympathetic action may set up in the other eye which can lead to total blindness.

Treatment

1   Close the eye and cover it with a pad, fixed in place with Sellotape (Scotch tape).

← Hold an eyepad in position with ordinary adhesive tape such as Sellotape or Scotch tape.

2   If the pain is severe cover the good eye as well.

3   Get the casualty to lie down and reassure him.

4   Give two paracetamol tablets for the pain, and repeat every four hours.

5   Make every effort to get the casualty to hospital as quickly as possible.

← If the pain is intense cover both eyes. Make sure the casualty is comfortable – if necessary, to ensure comfort, place a pad over the good eye as well as the bad eye before bandaging.

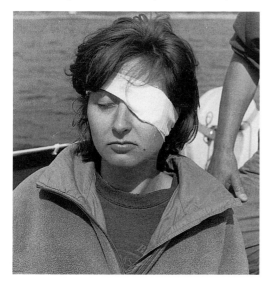

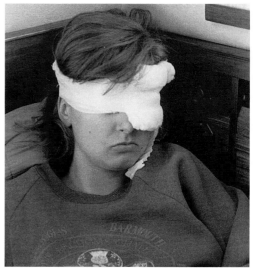

The outer, visible part of the ear is relatively unimportant as it is merely skin and cartilage. The important parts of the ear are deep inside the skull. The canal which leads to the inner parts of the ear is lined with skin and ends at the eardrum which is delicate and sensitive.

WOUNDS TO THE OUTER PART OF THE EAR

Treat as any other flesh wound (see page 34).

BLEEDING FROM THE EAR

After an injury to the skull there may be bleeding from the ear. If the casualty has had a knock on the head or trauma to the upper part of his body and you see blood coming from the ear you must find out where it is coming from.

Carefully and gently wipe away the blood from the outside part of the ear and watch to see where the blood is coming from. If you can see that it is coming from a wound on the fleshy part of the outer ear or the skin at the entrance to the ear canal treat it as an ordinary wound.

If you see that the blood is coming from deep inside the canal it may be coming from inside

the skull. This is serious, and you should treat the casualty as a head injury (page 28). Make every effort to get him to hospital as quickly as possible.

EARACHE

Earache may be caused by inequality of pressure on the two sides of the eardrum after diving or swimming. It may follow a head injury or blast, or it may be a symptom of middle ear infection.

Treatment
If you suspect that there is unequal pressure on the eardrum try to equalise it by asking the patient to hold his nose closed while inflating his cheeks and then swallowing.

If earache follows a blow to the head treat it as a head injury (see page 28).

If the pain follows a cold or sore throat, or there is no injury and the patient has not been swimming or diving, treat it as an infection. Rest the patient and give him two paracetamol tablets for the pain, repeated every four hours if necessary. If you are on an ocean passage and are carrying antibiotics, use them as directed.

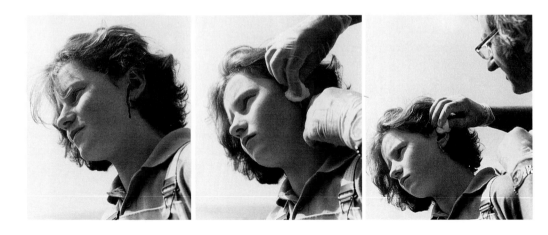

▲ Bleeding from the ear could be a sign of serious head injury.

Wipe the blood away – but remember to wear gloves . . .

And watch closely to see where the blood is coming from.

☛ To equalise pressure in the ears to relieve earache, hold your nose, inflate your cheeks and swallow.

FOREIGN BODY IN THE EAR

Small objects may lodge in the ear canal. Occasionally an insect will fly or crawl in and drive the casualty mad by buzzing next to the eardrum. In either case pour in a teaspoonful of tepid water or olive oil. This will often float out the object or the insect. Even if the insect does not float out it will be drowned and stop buzzing. If the foreign body does not float out, pour in one more teaspoonful.

Do not attempt to remove the object with tweezers or any other implement as you may damage the eardrum. It will do no harm to leave it there until you get medical help.

DEAFNESS

Sudden deafness after swimming is usually caused by wax in the ears. This can be treated by pouring a small quantity of tepid olive oil into the ear canal and allowing it to drain by lying or sitting with the head on one side. Do not attempt to shift the wax with a matchstick or you may damage the eardrum.

TOOTHACHE

1 Give two paracetamol tablets every four hours as long as the pain persists.

2 Place a warm compress – a flannel soaked in hot water – on the side of the face with the aching tooth.

DENTAL ABSCESS

A dental abscess in the early stages is a localised collection of pus at the base of a tooth which cannot escape, causing throbbing pain through a build up of pressure, and consequently the tooth will be tender to bite on. Treatment is to commence a course of antibiotics, if possible, and to seek professional help as soon as possible. In the interim, regular warm salt water mouth washes (one level teaspoon per tumbler) and analgesics should be taken.

LOST FILLINGS

A filling may become loose and drop out, leaving a hole in the enamel of the tooth. This may cause pain if the nerve is exposed or if the jagged edge of the tooth catches the cheek or gum. So if you are going to make a long ocean passage it is worthwhile taking a small dental kit which will enable you to put in a temporary filling.

1 Make up the filling material as directed in the instructions that come with the dental kit.

2 Place dental swabs or small rolls of dry gauze in the mouth around the tooth to absorb saliva, then make sure that the cavity is dry.

3 Use a small spatula to pack the filler into the cavity and smooth it off.

4 Leave it to harden by making sure the patient doesn't eat or drink for four hours.

SUGGESTED DENTAL KIT

- Temporary filling material
- Dental swabs
- Dental mirror
- Spatula

The Dentanurse dental kit provides everything you need for a temporary tooth repair.

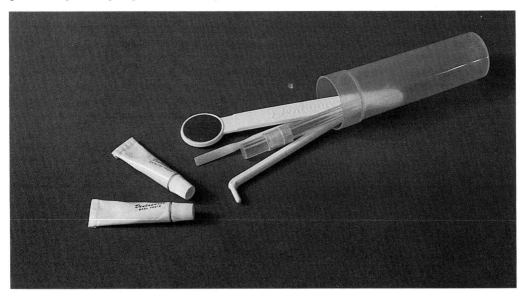

SICKNESS

During the first part of a pregnancy many women suffer bouts of sickness. The woman feels tired and nauseated as well as being sick. Obviously anyone who feels like this will be made worse by the motion of a small boat.

Treatment

1 Lie the patient down in a secure, airy, comfortable place and give her drinks to sip.

2 Leave the patient to rest. Let her sleep if she can.

3 Usually the patient will settle down after 24 hours. If she doesn't and is still being sick you must get her ashore to medical attention.

BLEEDING FROM THE VAGINA DURING PREGNANCY

Any bleeding from the birth canal during pregnancy is abnormal and should be treated as a type of internal bleeding as directed on page 58.

In addition place clean towels over the entrance to the vagina.

This is a serious emergency: the slightest bleeding may indicate the start of a miscarriage, which will lead to more serious bleeding. You must make every effort to get the patient ashore as quickly as possible. Use the radio to get advice and assistance.

WARNING

A woman in the early stages of pregnancy should not take any medication that has not been specifically prescribed for her by a doctor. Do not use seasickness pills or plasters unless the patient has discussed her pregnancy with a doctor who says that it is safe to use them.

ABDOMINAL PAIN IN PREGNANCY

Pain in the abdomen, especially the lower abdomen, may be caused by a complication of pregnancy or it may be a symptom of some unrelated illness. In either case it must be taken seriously.

Treatment

1 Place the patient in a secure, comofortable position. Usually the most comfortable is semi-lying with pillows under her shoulders and under her knees.

2 Do not give anything by mouth unless you are far offshore and cannot get to medical aid for hours.

3 If the pain persists for more than an hour make every effort to get the patient to medical attention as soon as possible. Use the radio to get advice and assistance.

It is not likely that a woman who is 40 weeks pregnant and therefore about to give birth will go to sea. However, many babies are born prematurely between 34 and 40 weeks. This section should enable you to deal with such an unexpected early birth.

The signs of labour beginning are abdominal pains and backache. There may be a discharge of blood and mucus from the birth canal. This discharge may be slight, but however slight the pains and the discharge are, you must do everything you can to get the mother to medical attention. Use the radio to get advice and call for help.

Preparation

1 If you think that the mother is starting labour make her rest in a secure place.

2 Make a cot for the baby from a box or drawer. Line it with clean dry towels or blanket. Prepare some clean dry cloths to wrap around the baby.

3 Boil a pair of scissors and three pieces of string each 23 cm (9 in) long to sterilise them.

4 Make up a delivery couch for the mother. Place an oilskin or waterproof sheet on the bed.

The birth of the baby

1 The labour may be a few minutes or hours, so keep trying to get medical assistance.

2 As the mother rests she will feel the contractions of her womb getting stronger and more frequent.

3 There may be a large discharge of watery fluid from the vagina. Wash around the entrance to the birth canal with water that has been boiled and then cooled. Cover the mother with a clean sheet.

4 When a baby is born it will take several contractions before the head of the baby is completely out of the birth canal. Support the head of the baby as it is born. Do not pull on it.

5 When the shoulders of the baby are born put your fingers under the baby's shoulders and guide it upwards over the mother's stomach. The baby will be slippery so hold firmly.

6 When the baby is out of the birth canal remember that he is still attached to the mother by the umbilical cord. Do not pull on the cord or stretch it. Hold the baby upside-down and he will start to breathe and possibly cry.

7 When the baby is breathing lay him against the mother's legs and cover him with a clean cloth.

8 Wait for the afterbirth to be born. Do not pull on the cord. Rub the skin of the mother's abdomen just below her navel, and this will help the womb to expel the afterbirth. Do not push; just rub gently. Keep the afterbirth for the doctor to examine when you get to medical aid.

Tying the umbilical cord
Look to see if the cord is pulsating. If it has stopped pulsating and the baby is breathing you may tie off the cord. Ideally it should not be tied until the afterbirth has come out, but if the afterbirth has not appeared after 15 minutes you may tie the cord.

1 Tie one of the boiled pieces of string around the cord about 15 cm (6 in) from the baby's abdomen.

2 Tie another piece about 20 cm (8 in) from the baby's abdomen. Make sure that the two pieces of string are tight around the cord and firmly knotted.

3 Cut the cord between the two pieces of string.

4 For extra safety tie another piece of string around the cord 5 cm (2 in) nearer the baby than the first piece.

Looking after the baby
The first essential is to keep the baby warm. Wrap him in clean dry cloths and put him into a sleeping bag with the mother nursing him. Cover the baby's scalp with a cloth so that only the face is bare.

Do not bother about feeding the baby for at least 24 hours.

Looking after the mother
Once the baby and the afterbirth are born wrap the mother in clean cloths. Put her into a sleeping bag and let her nurse the baby.

When the mother needs to sleep take the baby from her, see that he is well wrapped up and place him in the cot you have prepared.

Once the mother has had about six hours' rest encourage her to move about and walk a little to stretch her legs.

There is no more lonely place to be than on a small boat at sea when a medical emergency occurs. So as well as carrying out First Aid procedures it is essential that you communicate with shore-based organisations to get the maximum amount of help as quickly as possible for seriously ill or injured people.

To do this you must have technical skills so you can attract the attention of the emergency services, and once you have their attention you must give them full and accurate information so they can decide how best to assist you. Anyone who has worked in the emergency services will tell you that the most frustrating part of the job is trying to get aid to a casualty on the basis of incomplete or inaccurate information.

Communications are of two types. There are general distress signals which tell observers that you have a problem but not what the problem is. Secondly there are communications which give the category of the emergency or, in the case of the spoken word by radio telephone, precise details.

The full list of distress signals is given in Annex IV of the International Regulations for Preventing Collisions at Sea, and in nautical almanacs for yachtsmen.

A distress signal must be used only when a vessel or person is in serious and immediate danger and urgent help is needed. Remember that if you use a general distress signal the coastguard will initiate a major search-and-rescue operation at considerable cost, possibly putting the personnel of the rescue services at risk. I have tried to indicate throughout the book when a condition is serious enough to warrant a distress signal.

If you have a radio telephone there is no problem. Call a coastal radio station and ask for medical advice. Once the operator has all the information he needs he will either link you to a doctor who will advise you or he will initiate emergency action to bring help to you.

GENERAL DISTRESS SIGNALS

Flares
A red hand flare is visible at night and possibly in daylight for about three miles. If you are more than three miles from land or the nearest vessel you will need to use a rocket parachute flare.

In daylight an orange smoke signal is more visible than flares.

Light signals
At night you can flash a distress signal with a hand torch or searchlight. The international distress signal is the letters SOS, flashed in morse as · · · − − − · · · This is a general distress signal and does not tell the recipient that you have a medical emergency. However, it has the advantage that most people will recognise it as a distress signal and report it to the rescue services.

The international code signal W means "I require medical assistance" In morse code this is flashed as · − − (By daylight you could use the single international flag signal for W, or signal the letter W by semaphore.) Although this is a more specific way of getting help not everyone will recognise either the morse code or the international code, so in many cases you will have to use the general distress signal to attract attention.

◄ The semaphore signal for the letter W.

COMMUNICATIONS BY RADIO

Almost every small vessel now has a radiotelephone. Most boats have VHF, but those equipped for longer voyages will have MF or HF. VHF radio has a range that is slightly better than line-of-sight between the aerial transmitting and the aerial receiving; MF has a range of about 300 miles, while the range of HF is potentially worldwide.

Radiotelephones are a great boon for small-boat sailors, but you must always remember that however powerful the set and however many people hear you, it is the completeness and accuracy of your message that counts. This is especially true in an emergency, so before you begin a call make sure that you are ready with all the information that you will need.

You will have to give information about your vessel, then you will need to give information about the casualty.

➤ Ideally you should give your position as a distance and bearing FROM a prominent feature, but a lat/long position taken from the electronic navigator is also acceptable.

Information about the boat
- The name and type of your vessel.
- Its capabilities as to speed.
- The present position of your vessel either:
a) as latitude and longitude or
b) as distance off a fixed point with your true bearing from it.
- Your course and speed.
- Weather conditions at your position.
- Identifying characteristics of your vessel, such as sail or hull colour etc.
- What accommodation you have on board.
- List of contents of your First Aid kit.

Information about the casualty
- Age and sex
- If an accident has occurred, a brief description of the accident and the injuries received. Take a good look at the casualty so you can give details and indicate the severity of the injuries – is he conscious, and how much blood has he lost?
- If the casualty has been taken ill, a brief description of the symptoms. Any important facts about the patient's history – is he a diabetic, or is he already on medical treatment?

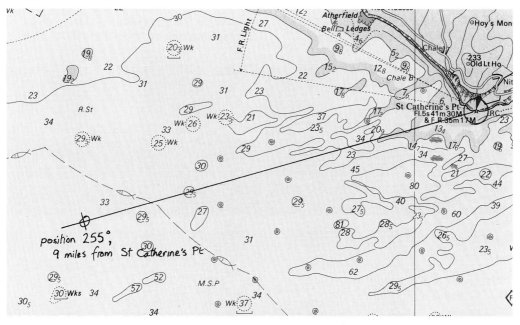

TRANSMITTING A MESSAGE IN A MEDICAL EMERGENCY

Setting up the radio

1 Identify your nearest Coast Radio Station. If you are not familiar enough with radio procedures to do this, you can transmit to 'All stations'.

2 If you are using VHF, switch on, select high power (25 W) and switch to Channel 16 (there will often be a special button for Channel 16).

3 If you are using MF radio transmit on 2182 kHz. On HF, transmit on 4125 kHz or 6215 kHz. You may transmit an urgency message at any time, but on the hour and half-hour there are three-minute silence periods on MF and HF for distress and urgency calls. So if you have not been able to get a reply, call again during a silence period.

4 Marine radios are usually of the Simplex type, which means you cannot transmit and receive at the same time. There will be a switch on the handset which you must press to transmit. When you have finished speaking you must release the switch or you will not be able to hear the response. Always say 'Over' before you release the switch.

The message

In a medical emergency you should send an 'urgency' or 'Pan-Pan' message, not a distress call. So:

1 Press the transmit switch and begin 'PAN-PAN MEDICO, PAN-PAN MEDICO, PAN-PAN MEDICO'.

2 Keep the switch depressed and say the name of the nearest Coast Radio Station three times.

3 If you do not know the name of a Coast Radio Station, or if you get no reply after your 'Pan-Pan Medico' call, say 'ALL STATIONS, ALL STATIONS, ALL STATIONS'.

4 Give the name of your vessel three times.

5 Say 'Over' and release the transmit switch.

6 You will hear the operator calling the name of your vessel. When he asks you to do so, give your message. Remember to press the transmit switch before you start talking.

7 When you have given all the information about your vessel and the casualty, say 'Over', release the transmit switch and listen. The operator will ask questions and will then tell

← Switch on the power at the boat switchboard . . .

Turn on the radio and select the emergency channel . . .

Press the switch on the microphone to transmit your message...

And release the switch to listen for a reply.

▲ If the emergency services are coming to you they will want to talk to you, so keep listening on the channel you have been using.

you what he is going to do. He will either connect you to a doctor or will alert the emergency services. Keep listening on the calling channel (Channel 16 on VHF) unless he tells you to change to another channel.

8 If you lose contact at any time, call again on the calling channel (Channel 16 on VHF).

9 Once the emergency services are coming to your assistance you must continue to listen on the channel you have been using, because the lifeboat coxswain or the helicopter pilot may want to speak to you.

Mobile telephones

It is tempting to use a mobile phone as your means of communication in an emergency, dialling the emergency services (999 in the UK) and asking for the Coastguard. The draw-back is that they will not be able to find your position by RDF (Radio Direction Finder), as they can if you are using VHF. Given time they may be able to find out which aerial received the transmission from your mobile, but this only gives a very approximate idea of your position. In addition, a mobile phone is not nearly as robust as a properly-fitted marine radio transmitter, and will deteriorate in wet and salty conditions.

Only use the mobile phone as an adjunct to the maritime radio, and not as a substitute.

Moving a casualty on a boat is made difficult by the motion of the boat and by the lack of space and equipment, and it is all too easy to add to his injuries while attempting to move him. Transferring casualties from vessel to vessel is also extremely hazardous.

So the basic rule is: **never move a casualty unless you have to.** Unless there is immediate danger to the casualty attend to him where he is, and wait for help.

When you have attended to him, decide whether you need to move him for comfort and security. If you do, prepare the place for him, then decide how you can best move him.

MOVING A CASUALTY ON THE VESSEL

If you have to get a casualty who cannot stand out of danger quickly, use the *drag carry*. If the casualty can stand but is unsteady use the *human crutch* method. If the casualty has to be carried and you are the only First Aider, use the *fireman's lift* method. This is a difficult carry, and potentially dangerous on a boat

← The drag carry.

because once the casualty is on your shoulder the centre of gravity is high, which makes it difficult to keep steady on a rolling vessel.

Drag carry
1 Fold the casualty's arms across his chest with him lying face up.

2 Put your hands underneath his shoulders resting his head on your forearms.

3 Lift his shoulders off the floor and drag him backwards.

← For the fireman's lift, raise the casualty to her knees . . .

Then to her feet. Bend down and put your arm around her waist.

Let her flop across you and put your right arm around her legs.

Human crutch

1   Stand next to the casualty facing the same way. Get the casualty to put his arm around your neck.

2   Hold the casualty's hand (the one around your neck) with your outside hand, and put your other arm around his waist.

3   You can now walk together, and the casualty also has a free hand to steady himself with.

Fireman's lift

1   Stand facing the casualty, put your arms under his arms and clasp your hands together at his back. Raise him to his knees and then to his feet.

2   Take hold of his right wrist with your left hand, bend down so that your right shoulder is level with his lower abdomen and allow him to fall across your shoulder. Place your right arm around his legs.

3   Stand up and take the casualty's right wrist into your right hand. You now have your left hand free to steady yourself.

← The human crutch technique for the walking wounded. Note that the casualty has a free hand to steady herself.

Stand up!

Take the casualty's right arm and bring it round to yours.

Hold her right hand in yours, and you will have a hand free.

Stretchers

If there is more than one First Aider and there is time, the best way to move a casualty is on an improvised stretcher.

Take two sailing jackets or overtrousers and put the dinghy oars through the arms or legs. Make sure that they will take the weight of the casualty. Then secure the casualty on the stretcher, making sure that his elbows and head are protected. You can now carry him safely.

▶ You can improvise a stretcher from a couple of sailing jackets and a pair of oars from the dinghy. Try putting the oars through the arms and zipping the jackets around them.

◄ The lifeboat crew arrive with a Neil Robertson stretcher.

The crew check the casualty lying in the cockpit.

They strap her limbs together to secure them . . .

◄ With the casualty secure, the crew begin the transfer.

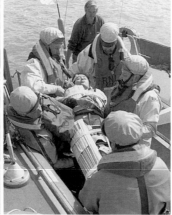

They manoeuvre the stretcher over the rails . . .

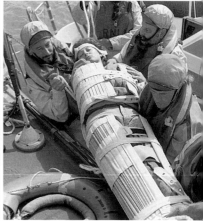

And onto the coachroof of the lifeboat by the cabin hatch.

TRANSFER FROM SHIP TO SHIP

Never do this unless you have to, because it is an extremely hazardous procedure during which the casualty can receive further injuries or even drown.

If a lifeboat is coming alongside, leave the casualty in a secure position until the doctor, First Aiders or crew come aboard your vessel to assess the situation.

If you have to transfer a casualty wait until you can use the Neil Robertson stretcher carried on the lifeboat. Protect the head of the casualty.

← If help is at hand, simply make the casualty comfortable and secure, and wait.

If you have a casualty with a suspected back or neck injury **do not** move him until have expert help and if possible the proper equipment.

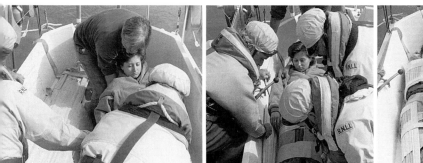

And move her onto the stretcher laid out on the other bench.

They carefully place her on the stretcher . . .

And secure its reinforced sides around her.

A quick check to make sure all is well . . .

And they lower her down the hatch . . .

Into the cabin where she can be given medical attention.

Survival is the art of maintaining life in a hostile environment. To do this means maintaining body temperature, adequate body fluid and a minimum amount of energy, while overcoming any injury or illness. People survive best if they are well prepared, if they have the knowledge and skills to perform the necessary tasks for survival and if they have the will to carry on.

There are two types of disaster that can overcome a small vessel and put the survival of her crew in doubt. In the first the boat is left powerless owing to engine failure, lack of wind or dismasting. You still have the vessel to shelter on, but you will have to spend much longer at sea than you expected to.

In this case you should be able to sit out the emergency, even if you have no radio to call for help (make sure you have an emergency aerial for use in case of dismasting). The golden rule is for everyone on board to stay with the vessel; it is a cardinal error for somebody to try to swim ashore. The most important thing in this situation is to keep your

→ Your boat may seem to be wrecked beyond hope of repair, but as long as she stays afloat she is your best liferaft.

nerve, to use all the equipment that you have on the vessel and to stay with the vessel as long as you possibly can.

In the second and more serious type of disaster the vessel actually sinks. In this case you will have to survive with much less equipment and you will be in a dinghy or liferaft, but the basic rules still apply.

PREPARATION FOR SURVIVAL

Before you set out on any passage you must make sure that you have the emergency equipment appropriate for the scale of the voyage.

You must have a liferaft if you are going offshore. It must have been serviced within the recommended time and it must contain the specified emergency equipment. But this alone will not ensure your survival, and if you have a few moments before your ship sinks under you, you should use that time to gather together a few useful items before you abandon ship. So let's look at what survival actually entails so that we can decide what the most important pieces of equipment are.

Maintaining body temperature

Cold can kill very quickly. At sea in latitudes higher than 50 degrees it is often cold during the day, and for most of the year very cold at night. Even in lower latitudes it is often very cold at night, especially if there is a clear sky. The body loses heat by convection caused by the wind, evaporation of sweat, conduction to colder surroundings and by radiation. What you need to prevent such heat loss is adequate insulation.

The best insulation is several layers of dry clothing, with a waterproof outer layer which will deflect the wind as well as keep you dry. Heat is lost very quickly through wet materials because water is a good heat conductor. Make sure that you have the best possible footwear and take a head covering such as a balaclava to wear under your hood. Put these clothes on as soon as possible so that although you may be too hot you will keep dry.

In a hot climate you will need to keep cool, but remember that it gets cold at night so take lots of clothing with you.

Maintaining body fluids

The body needs a minimum fluid intake even when inactive; it runs out of water well before it runs out of food reserves, so try to take as much watery fluid with you as possible. If you are properly clothed and still have a few minutes left, partially fill several containers with drinking water and attach them to the liferaft. If they are only partially filled they will float. In this way you can take a fair amount of water with you.

Overcoming injury and illness

In a survival situation it is likely that a crew member will be injured, and in the days after leaving the vessel someone may become ill. So it is essential to take a First Aid kit with you into the liferaft.

Keeping a minimal First Aid kit in a grab bag is a sound idea, so if there is only time to take the one bag it will contain the most essential items. Be sure to have seasickness remedies in the

← To stay warm you need plenty of dry wool covered with a waterproof outer layer. It is always colder than you expect.

grab bag, because even the hardest sailor is likely to become seasick in a liferaft. By far the best preparation to have is Scopaderm TTS as the plasters will become effective even if the patient has started to vomit. Take antibiotics in the bag – I recommend ciprofloxacin, a wide-spectrum antibiotic that is particularly useful for gastro-intestinal infections which add to dehydration. Add paracetamol tablets and Anthisan cream for sunburn and burns, and you have a minimal First Aid kit.

Maintaining minimal energy

It takes a long time for the body to exhaust its reserves of food, but it is a good idea to have some emergency rations with you. Chocolate and biscuits and high-energy foods which are easy to throw into the liferaft are useful.

LAUNCHING THE LIFERAFT

◆ Secure the painter and throw the canister or valise overboard . . .

◆ Yank the painter to trigger the inflator . . .

◆ The liferaft will inflate itself, remaining dry inside and the right way up . . .

◆ Ready to step into if your boat disappears from under you.

SURVIVAL TECHNIQUES

Once you are in a survival situation think of the four principles above and work towards them constantly.

Maintaining body temperature

Try to rig a shelter if you haven't got one. Make sure the liferaft canopy protects you as much as possible. The aim is to keep the wind off you, to keep as dry as possible and, at the other extreme, to have shade from the sun.

Try to maintain adequate clothing for the conditions. Try to remain as dry as possible as you get into the liferaft, and wear clothing which will keep you warm and dry.

In very hot climates you will need to cool yourself: you can use seawater to sponge yourself down, and the evaporation of the water will cool you and preserve your body fluid. Stay in the shade. Always anticipate changes of temperature, and if it is going to get cold at night dress for it early.

Maintaining body fluids

Take stock of your available fluid straight away, and try to ration it so that you will have a regular small intake for several days. In a cold climate one pint per day will be a reasonable intake. In a hot climate this amount will be sufficient if shade and cooling with seawater are used to reduce sweating.

If you can get organised to catch fish they will provide fluid as well as a little food value.

The question which has been asked for years is 'should I drink seawater?' The official answer is no. Certainly if you exhaust your supplies of fresh water over a period of days so that you become relatively dehydrated and then start to drink seawater you will quickly become ill. Some survivors have suggested that if you know that you are going to be self-sufficient with little fresh water for many days, you should start to use seawater from the start. If you do this you must not drink more than 800 mls per day, and you must drink it a few mouthfuls at a time spread out through the 24 hours. Some have added 40 per cent seawater to their fresh water from the start, others have drunk fresh water one day, and seawater the next. The Robertson family gave each other seawater enemas using the tube of the pump and a plastic bag.

One thing is certain: you should only use these methods if you know that you are facing many days without fresh water. For most people it will be sufficient to take extra water and ration it carefully.

As soon as you are in a dinghy or liferaft you must begin to collect rainwater as soon as you can. If you fill all your containers, drink several pints while the rain is falling rather than not collect it at all. This will ensure that you are well hydrated.

Illness

If you have to take to a liferaft or other small craft everyone should apply a Scopaderm TTS anti-seasickness plaster. It is important to avoid seasickness because it adds to dehydration, it is miserable and reduces morale and effectiveness.

If anyone develops diarrhoea they should be given two Ciprofloxacin tablets twice a day for three days. This will work quickly and will prevent dehydration.

Also published by Fernhurst Books

For a free full-colour brochure write, phone or fax us at:
Fernhurst Books, Duke's Path, High Street, Arundel
West Sussex, BN18 9AJ, UK
Tel: 01903 882277   Fax: 01903 882715